I Have Need of the Poets

*A Seventh
CSS Publications
Anthology*

© Copyright 1984 by Rebecca S. Bell and C. Sherman Severin
CSS Publications, P.O. Box 23, Iowa Falls, Iowa 50126

ISBN: 0-942170-07-5

I Have Need of the Poets

Edited by
Rebecca S. Bell

CSS Publications Staff

Rebecca S. Bell
Editor-in-Chief & Co-Publisher
Des Moines, Iowa

C. Sherman Severin
Business Manager & Co-Publisher
Lake Oswego, Oregon

Curt L. Sytsma
Editorial Adviser
Des Moines, Iowa

Gladys L. Bell
Office Manager
Iowa Falls, Iowa

A special thanks to:
Mike Bell
The Iowa Falls Gang
The Poetry Judges
Doug Scott
Margaret Wagner
Alexis Mitchell

*This book is lovingly dedicated
to Walter L. Pritchard,
a shining soul with a soaring spirit*

I Have Need
of the Poets

I have need of the poets
and of their powerful solace
gentling into my tremulous soul
and of their sorrows
trickling through each
  of my thorny vertebrae
To strengthen my buckling spine
I have need of some potent measure
  of their passionate fluids
some sentient potion for each pithy chakra

Barbara McCorkhill
Akron, Ohio

"Fedalma entered, cast away the cloud
Of serge and linen, and, outbeaming bright,
Advanced a pace towards Silva."

Introduction
A Pace Towards Silva

They want me today. Just as I was supposed to write an introduction to another poetry anthology, they want me. One of my clients claims that forty jobs are at stake — and he's right, of course. Another's right to be a mother to her daughter is at stake — and she's right as well. There are so many needs in this need-ridden world, and I have my own. That's why I have need of the poets.

It was Goethe, you know, who said that "(p)oetry is the universal possession of mankind, revealing itself everywhere, and at all times. . . ." It *is* my possession — not because I have any right to fancy myself especially entitled, but because poetry is like the rising sun — the uncommon wealth in the common domain. The only warrant you need to experience that wealth is the wit to want to, and the only title you need is your humanity.

One of the greatest conundrums in human history can only be answered by a bifurcated tautology: A poet is a person who writes poetry, and poetry is that which is written by a poet.

Absurd, you say? Not really. Why did Ortega Gasset

define poetry as fermented adolescence, as though such a feeling were really a definition? Why did Bodenheim define poetry as "the impish attempt to paint the color of the wind"? Why, indeed? Except, perhaps, that poetry is the universal reflection of our need to be human in an inhuman world — our need for people who measure values by tugs at the soulthrob.

In this world, CSS Publications is a wonder. Its initials are similar to my own, and sometimes I have reason to suspect that its patrons consider me their benefactor. I only wish. CSS is a dream that preceded me and a dream that will just as certainly outlive me, if only because it is devoted to the ultimate chakra in our emotional backbone — our need to share our feelings.

Some years ago, I was asked to preside at the first CSS Publications Poetry Banquet — commemorating, as I recall, their third anthology. I thought it was an honor, but the real honor was the presence of poets from around the nation. I knew then what I know now — that CSS was and is an elegant forum for the discovery of wildflowers in the back woods, for the discovery of the exquisite beauty of fool's gold on a gravel road, for the discovery of what matters — the best of us that is all of us.

CSS Publications is now publishing its seventh anthology and its ninth book of poetry. I have become bound to it — not as I am bound to one of my clients as an attorney, but as a poet is bound to his own. Consider it: Where else can you find a book devoted to the poems that please us because they reflect the poets who *are* us? Poetry is not a matter of meter or form; it is the sixth and highest sense, and our poets are those who have the daring to experience — and share — it.

In this seventh anthology, CSS has done the remarkably sensible: It has defined its chapters by *poets*. Consider that!

Not by themes (do we have another poem on a barn?); not by emotions *per se* (do we have another poem that cries its heart out for the "despair" chapter?); not by anything but the only universal — the uncommon wealth in the common domain.

Chapter 1 is William Shakespeare, purging the English language of its pretensions and elevating it to higher heights by dramatising the emotions that are common to us all. Chapter 2 is Robert Burns, the satirical, lyrical, fanciful ambassador to lust. Chapter 3 is A.E. Housman, the man whose lust was frustrated and who found his common bond in an uncommon recognition of the beauty of agony.

Chapter 4 is Gertrude Stein, will incarnate — incomprehensible, free-flowing, belligerent, eternal will. Chapter 5 is Oscar Wilde, the heart yielding to the will, as *De Profundis* sacrificed the satirist. Chapter 6 is Thomas Moore, satirical but free, alive in an age when poets could almost make a living by being poets and by striving for the universal dreams.

Chapter 7 of the seventh anthology is the most important of all. It is Walt Whitman. It is poetry growing from the heartland and emanating across the world in its cosmic consciousness. It is the revelation of the grandeur of the common, the theme of democracy. It is also the theme of CSS Publications.

I am not CSS Publications. Would to God I were because I believe that there is nothing any man or woman could do that should more endear them to our common humanity than just such an endeavor as this.

— *Curt L. Sytsma*
Des Moines, Iowa
August, 1984

Chapter 1

2	Unanswered	Clo Weirich
3	Skeleton Seated in the Middle of a Plaza	Ivan Arguelles
4	Threnody	Andrew Dawson
5	The Hermit Scholar	Janet Marie
6	Spaces Invisible	Stephen Whyte
7	Nightmare	Wilfred M. Johnson
8	In Evil Voices	Jean A. Stanford
9	Driving Through Fog	Ron MacLean
10	Seven Heights Within	Averi Torres
11	Emulate	Lynne A. Chapman

Chapter 2

14	Mindworks	Mary Himka Young
15	Violation	J. Karyl Arnold
15	Saying Hello	Karen Black
16	A Chance Meeting After School	Ron MacLean
17	Rain Fell Flat on the Windshield	Kim Kolker
18	Meeting You	Meg Kramer
18	No Goodbye	Tammy Rayne Abbey
19	A Dream	Tina Abolins
20	Macho Melon	Pat King
21	Climate	Charles Fabrizio
22	Crosscountry	Sarah P. Simmons
24	Mind Control	Renee Ingledue
25	The Light in My Eyes is You	Roger Wilbur
26	Once Again	Mike Mihaljevich
26	Night Visitor	Marie Grant
27	The Sound of Boots	Jack Bernier

Chapter 3

30	Pre-Boarding Call	Joan Edwards
31	Woman	Judith Lewis von Buchler
32	Shelf Life	Jeff T. Dick
33	Visitor	Glenda Winders
34	Rebirth	Caroline St. Julien
35	Anxiety	LaMoyne Nations
36	Slot Machine	J. M. Frank
37	Sundays	Jill King
38	Proletarii	Laurre Breman
39	Poor Hygiene	Jeff Wright
39	Inconscient	Arthur C. Frick
40	Cobweb	Frances R. Johnson
41	Preserving 17 Years of Marriage In a Savage Jungle	Dale Bryant
42	The Mother Dreams	Brian Finney
43	In the City	Jim Albright
43	39th Street Elementary School	Jack Bernier
44	Confusion	Jennifer Dongvillo
44	Snow Storm	Jennifer Riddle Cupples
45	Waiting for Tigers	Maxine Follstad
45	Last Bus for Timbuktu	Linda J. Reed
46	The Turning Away	Margaret Brady
49	The Drowning (to the novelist, Virginia Woolf)	Martha K. Graham
50	Mother's Nursing Home Roommate	Jerri Evans
51	Grief	Enid M. Bennett
52	John	Virgil Chabre
53	Worlds Apart	Ron MacLean

Chapter 4

56	The Old Men	Conrad Simonson
57	In God's Image	Ann J. Majure
58	Anger	Michael Felsburg
58	Mistakes	Chema Ude
59	Solomon On High	Mike Eldon
60	The Minstrel	June L. Shipley
61	To Stephen King	Marie Asner
62	Poet's Prayer to His Muse	E. Wright
63	A Complaint Addressed to W.B. Yeats	Will C. Jumper
64	Anguish and Ecstacy	Alice Mackenzie Swaim
65	Ann Sexton	Linda Curtis
66	The Survivor	Laurre Breman
67	Cat-Scan	Ivan Arguelles
68	In the Meantime	Esther Edleman
68	Last Years	Frances H. Hughes
69	Midgard	Ronald L. Andrzejewski
70	Winter Comes	J. M. Frank
71	Picasso	Frances R. Johnson
72	Long Abandoned, Yet It Still Stands	Sheryl Carlon
72	The Chestnut Tree	Sherrill Morgan Finn
74	Staigue Fort, Ireland	Ann Caroline Kabel
75	To Sacajawea at Riverton	Kay Jons Roelfsema

Chapter 5

78	Love Song for My Native State	Joan Merryman Burns
79	Plains Summer	Eleanor Mader
80	Bathroom Alien	Doris T. Brokaw
80	Garden Follies	Mildred Hope Wood
81	Imprints	Clo Weirich
81	Pre-Dawn Vigil	Myrtle T. Cavallo
82	Identity	Jean Marie Schultz
83	The Peach Tree Blooms	IvaNelle Simak
84	Remembrance	Jean Lollich Warner
84	My Mother	Esther Edleman

85	For Papa, The Last Time	Lynne Proctor Sancken
86	Growing Sweetcorn	Lynne Proctor Sancken
87	Evening Sonnet	Michael Gfoeller
87	To Dale	Meg Kramer
88	Caring	R. J. Caylor
89	Certainty	Catherine Boulanger
89	Benevolence	Aaron Koch
90	Something Blue	Dorothy J. Turnour
91	We're All Parents Now	Noni Bookbinder Bell
92	Mother's Song to Newborn	Maxine Follstad
92	Dreams	Mary Pagliaro
93	Someday, My Little One	Kay Logsdon Pearce
94	Walk	Mary Himka Young
95	I'll Miss You	Margery Disburg
96	In the Little House	William P. Riddle
97	Mother's Day — 1984	Justin Mitchell Sytsma
98	Rocking Chair Frame	Sharon L. Buettell
99	Dad and Dominoes	Marsha A. Mitchell
100	The Physics of Ten	Jean Kennedy
101	Horseshoe Luck	Jean Kennedy
102	On Giving a Saint Christopher Medal	Pat King
103	When My Daughter Visits	Delores Mundell
104	Twins	Ann S. Walters
105	To You, Away	Minneh M. Karanja
106	The Fun House	Linda Lee Curtis
106	Inheritance	Mary Hamilton Neary
107	Thanks for My Unfriend	Corinne B. Ansell
107	Damned If You Do	Dean M. LeBel
108	Three Traditional Kabyle Songs	
		Charlotte H. Bruner, Translator
110	Deer Season	Ethel Case Cook
110	Counterpoint	J. Karyl Arnold
111	Bittersweet	Barbara Kee Vatovec
111	Solo Flight	Jennifer Becker
112	When Gone the Flame	Nancy Brier O'Neal
112	Insomnus	Krista Werner
113	Like A Single Leaf	Janet Rahmani
114	Unruly Intruder	Alice Makenzie Swaim
115	Within Depression's Grasp	Betty Jane Sachara
116	Disintegration	Karla J. Ziesemer

Chapter 6

118	Anniversary	*Kathleen W. Ela*
119	Vigil	*Christine Christian*
120	Prayer Over An Old Photograph	*Sherrill Morgan Finn*
121	Pax Tecum Et Lux Eterna	*Will C. Jumper*
122	Alone	*Elizabeth Welden*
122	Stars	*Jennifer Ryan*
123	October Rose	*Sister Monica Lammers*
124	Of Robes for Rituals	*Alice Mackenzie Swaim*
124	The Sun	*Andrew Corson*
125	Ghost Moon	*Beth Helen Nowell*
126	Salute to America Upon the Fourth of July: An Immigrant Remembers	*Patricia J. Hoad*
127	Hope	*J. M. Frank*
127	Dawn Flight	*Arthur C. Frick*
128	Glacier	*Jim Albright*
128	Risk	*Arthur C. Frick*
129	Frostfire	*Frank Tropea*
130	An Image of Spring	*Tracy Grandy*
130	Signs of Spring	*Douglas Pfeiffer*
131	Butterfly	*Wayne C. Burgess*
131	God's Living Jewel	*Alex A. Widicker*
132	Rose Lawn Cemetery	*Margaret Brady*
133	Flash	*Jason Hobson*
134	Transition	*Leslie H. Fishel, Jr.*
134	Waterfall Variations	*Julie Stratton*
135	Bedtime	*Sara Sheppard Szymanski*
135	Contentment	*Sarah Jacquish*
136	The Dancer	*Lisa M. Billman*

136	Poem for the New York City Ballet	
		Claudia Hochberg
137	Child at the Symphony	Darrell H. Bartee
138	Sea Wife, Waiting	Jessie Eastman Holt
139	Bearance	Dorothy Moore
140	The Paper Court	E. Matthew Lewis
141	Becoming	Bonnie L. Thomas
142	From Out of the Blue	Vernelia B. Jobe
142	Dawn Flight	Arthur C. Frick
143	Night Surf	Kathryn Gelander
143	Aging	Meg Kramer
144	Within My Shut Eyes	Jean Kennedy
144	Patterns in the Sand	Christy Revnell
145	Gone Was My Night	Maude C. Booth
146	Springfire	Dolly Redden

Chapter 7

148	The Fire Next Time	Conrad Simonson
149	Ships Waiting at Vung Tao — Circa 1966	
		Dennis Torres
150	The Locked Ward	Ann Caroline Kabel
151	Snow	Andrew Corson
152	Requiescat	Caroline St. Julien
153	Motifs	Caroline St. Julien
154	Cain's Children	Jessie Eastman Holt
155	The Postlude	Jeff Wright

Judges — 156
Contributors — 158
CSS Publications — 167

Chapter 1

Unanswered

What strange planetary motion
sets us up for all elements
of our relationship
with one another

Does geometry of sorts
form figures within us
triangles of fear/hate
circles of love/trust

Are world waters waiting
to unleash wild energy
that could throw us
back into primordial slime

Can you imagine furious flames
stripping forested areas
that have taken milleniums
to reach maturity

Will the force of gravity
pull us apart
throw us to the stars
for an encounter
never to be filmed

As I hear these questions
puzzle pieces inside me
refuse to mesh
I find scattered patterns
of racial memories in disarray

Answer me
   earth/air
   fire/water
I am tired
of asking questions

Clo Weirich
Sioux City, Iowa

Skeleton Seated in the Middle of the Plaza

there is no poem inside me
only a white shell fragment
which the birds have picked at
over the centuries
I am studying music
because I cannot hear it
though I understand it is everywhere
the sun is an amiable beast
no matter how blood-stained he is
and the moon which shines
sometimes through my ribs
is the very source of metallurgy
the music I am studying
is the one of spheres
I have longings to be as dust
revolving on the calcinated planet
if I smile it is because I think
I hear the very first note
like rust descending from the heavens
so much commotion and no noise!
I know where the sky goes
when everything else has died
but I yearn for eyelids
and sleep long and everlasting
rather than to have to sit here
amid the wild congress of bodies

there is no song inside me
only the empty shape of a former sea
like the memory of the memory
of a flower that I used to be

Ivan Argüelles
Berkeley, California

Threnody

And when the opportunity comes to you
Sit with death awhile;
A long while if you can.

See the bloodlessness,
Hear the serenity,
Feel the slight.

Don't believe.

And then see,
Hear and
Feel again;
Only . . .
Cooler.

Touch death with your slow curious fingers.
Feel for the breath
That nostrils once caressed.
Count the pulse.
Remember the heartbeat.

Wonder.

Open the room's curtains
And give death sight.
Let the cold light of a gray day
See death.

(See the sores;
They don't bleed anymore;
The scars aren't ugly now)
You're still here.

(He won't talk to you.
He doesn't care about you anymore.
He doesn't see the bay and the sunset.
He doesn't dream now.)
Can you stand it?

Yes . . . yes,
Sit with death
Awhile.

Andrew N. Dawson
Key Largo, Florida

The Hermit Scholar
— after a viewing in the Dillon Galleries,
Metropolitan Museum of Art.

The true hermit scholar
fishes for fish, not fame.

His painting poetry
is a heart print.

In a Sung dynasty painting,
gibbons attack a heron's nest.

On Bantam River, a blue heron
stands like a sentinel,

flies away and reappears around
the next bend, waving calligraphy.

That blue heron rises, perches high
in a tree, gray as a fossilized

rock in China. It leads us down
the river to its mouth vanishing.

The transparent river reveals
its inner life to a hermit scholar.

Turtles, as though hypnotized,
sun on rocks, not one muscle flinching.

Sunfish and yellow perch glide by
waterlilies, pickerel weed, moss
on logs in tide pools.

Fish swim so readily
in their own element,

dart away when the fisherman's
canoe intrudes.

An October moon in its cradle,
gliding down the page of
an illuminated manuscript,

on water mosaic tiles
of green and burgundy,

a hermit scholar manages the river,
reclaiming what is his own.

Janet Marie
Hopewell, New Jersey

Spaces Invisible

Locked in a room
walls to save people from people
enemies everywhere inside us
as we smile and verbally stroke
a face or a wallet

All doors are closed
hearts, minds, and ears
like a prison cell within
cold barriers
that will not let an idea — Fly
enter or escape
without being swatted
by a wrinkled cliche

Chill in the caverns
bleakest, black despair
red in inward agression
manifesting itself with dynamite
stones caving in
blocking the route to escape
and knowledge that we are sun

Safe within the parlor
pressing clay against clay
molecules warming up
bodies breathing pleasure
wishing to touch souls

Dream in ivory tower
pen burning in blue
then singing in sighs
isolation reaches out
waves of compassion
clouds of sympathy

a star shone unreachable
touches the desert heart
and maybe, just maybe
its sun will open every door
and all souls will touch

Stephen Whyte
St. Louis, Missouri

Nightmare

Tormentor of my mind,
   cauldron in my brain
      where past,
         present
           and future
needle suspicion and fear.
   You search my attic,
      cellar
         and sewer.
You are terror without rules,
      pity
         or pardon.
   Your torture peers
      through closed eyes,
   as you probe
        my naked soul.

Wilfred M. Johnson
North Mankato, Minnesota

In Evil Voices

Shattered fragments
of broken moon
fall dormant
on my head.
Blackness all around me,
I lie silent
on my bed.
Waiting, watching . . .
the bright pieces
of shattered moon
seem to fall
in slow motion.
The stars
seem to taunt me.
Their laughter
is piercing
to my ears
and I cover them
with trembling hands.
I scream out
to the heavens;
in evil voices
they answer me,
"Silence, my child,
for now
You must sleep
and bring rest
to your weary soul!"
Tomorrow will begin
with the sun.

Jean A. Stanford
Wisconsin Dells, Wisconsin

Driving through Fog

A silent scream
rips my aching chest,
the cry of a soul anguished,
hating the pain of what I see
as time wasted; as though
a giant clock in my mind
is loudly ticking off seconds
and great things are being left undone.

Water squirts up from the tires,
and the windshield wipers pound out
their familiar pattern against the rain,
never winning, but never really losing.
Driving through the fog and mist,
enjoying the harmony of sounds,
and hating the idea that
I cannot see my destination,
I learn patience.

Alone in a field
far from myself and
far from the world,
I can shut off the clock.
Is it gaining perspective or running away?
That I don't know,
and the unanswered question
starts the clock to ticking again.

Ron MacLean
Monterey Park, California

Seven Heights Within

We have seven choices
how fortunate we are

When the doors are before us
we stand humbled
aware of ourselves
and
aware of what is beyond the doors

To choose the highest avenue
to choose the greatest thing in this world
that is the door
leading to spiritual awakening
to challenges
to growth
to rising very high

We have the choice always
of
walking through the door
into a new
and
beautiful existence
a bright shining white light
leading the way
or walking through the second door
a little dimmer light
perhaps a longer route
but one to also experience
and treasure, remembering that

Always, once inside
peaking comes
then the plateau
and again
we face the doors
and another choice

Throws of disrest
desire
energized from the Divine Source
create the passion to open the doors
to climb to greater heights
to scale mountain peaks
to caress the shining white light

Seven chances
Seven plateaus
How fortunate we are
to find
our seven layers within
leading to
God.

Averi Torres
Malibu, California

Emulate

We seek, we need, we strive.
We learn, we grow, we survive.
We find, we understand, we give.
We hope, we love, we live.

Lynne A. Chapman
Wolcott, New York

Chapter 2

Mindworks

Amid the blaring missives
and the piercing stares,
you've exposed your ears to a vacuum,
and your conscious to the unaware;
shoved down the cliffs of thought
to the shallow waters below
to be splattered into the blue
of dreams.

Gone is the nurturing
of the fetus of fear.
He cavorts about so healthily,
philosophizing with all thoughts near;
pushed through the tunnel of change
to the side unknown
to be led into the openness
of age.

So, rests your captor unceasingly,
determined to surround
your dreams, your pleasure, your important work,
especially in the evening hours;
fed into the grinding machine
of your pre-occupation
to be among the disciples
of lust.

Mary Himka Young
Wixom, Michigan

Violation

Lightning
with a hot bolt
raped the maple
on the tree lawn
at midnight.
Now she stands alone
in the August aftermath
shivering in sunlight,
stripped barkbare,
her covering and her dignity
like clothes shredded into rags
and scattered on the ground.

J. Karyl Arnold
Medina, Ohio

Saying Hello

We drift aimlessly
like ships
into proximity
of each other's harbor.
We exchange cargo
from time to time,
lightening each other's load.
We pass
in the sea of life.
Blink signals
and resume course.

Karen Black
Clear Lake, Iowa

A Chance Meeting After School

"Hello," he spoke shyly,
and her radiant smile surprised him;
a smile as though she'd just been
shown something extraordinary, like
a rainbow or a crimson sunset or
a budding rose; or just a
beet-faced, freckled smile,
and her response warmed his heart.

Staring at the ground,
he wonders what to say
to tell her how he's thought of her,
how deeply he wants to see this rose bloom.
He fumbles on his words while she watches,
perplexed, hoping he'll just talk —
but what to say?

The moment is passing and
the rose, so quick to bud,
begins to fade.
She giggles, he flushes,
angered at his inability to
hold the conversation he's dreamed
so many times.
He knows she's right to laugh,
that it's all rather silly
but that doesn't keep the rose from wilting,
the petals falling like rocks
thud thud thud thud
echo in his mind and
pound into his heart.

Ron MacLean
Monterey Park, California

Rain Fell Flat on the Windshield

Rain fell flat on the windshield
Like an old song heard too many times.
We sat together
For the first time,
Hesitant, afraid of pain.
Things had been easier
When our friendship was in pen, on paper.
But life is not real
When imprisoned in easiness.
Words came slowly and quietly.
Silences fell like feathers.

Leaving was hard;
We searched for reasons to remain within
The timeless cocoon we had spun,
Finding always one more piece of ourselves to give.
We finally parted when the rain had ceased to fall,
Our fingers lingering, touching warmth,
Reluctantly releasing.
There was no sudden technicolor rainbow stretched across the sky
To mark the time we had spent as beautiful,
But there should have been.

Kim Kolker
San Diego, California

Meeting You

Meeting you, I babble inconsequential nothings,
Having intended to divulge my deepest yearnings
And to mouth philosophical truths.
My tongue loosens as if I had sipped
A glass of sparkling champagne.
I am light-headed
Tasting the heady wine of your nearness.
I laugh too easily,
Chatter too frantically.
I dread the ebb of this exhilaration
And the certain depression that comes
When the glass is empty,
When the wine is gone.

Meg Kramer
Truman, Minnesota

No Goodbye

So much for long goodbyes,
   or short goodbyes,
      or any goodbyes at all.

We never even said hello.

You were just here,
   and I was here,
      and I laughed.

But we never said goodbye.

You were just gone,
   and I was alone,
      and I cried.

Tammy Rayne Abbey
Crosby, Minnesota

A Dream

. . . i dreamt of you last night.
why can't i remember your face?

   the park was hazy and glaring in confusion
but i caught you in a glimpse
of my unfocused memory.
   i reached for you with my eyes
and your aura became real.
our contours embraced
and i admitted aloud that i was in love
. . . with a stranger . . . you.
   we were holding hands
while talking to faces called friends.

   i am real inside
   i was a part of you
   complete
in an incomplete dream . . .

   and i remember
being in a room with only you.
our silent passion turned into soft flesh.
my fruitful mouth fed your hunger.
but then you were about to leave,
and i reached for you
and kissed your naked shoulder.
you fell into my arms,
telling me how wonderful i felt . . .

   you disappeared
into daylight,
your face ruffled away
into a river of void.
   where are you?
   who can you be?

Tina Abolins
Des Moines, Iowa

Macho Melon

He laughs but never plays the fool
talks but never tells too much
takes knocks but never flinches
feels her up
but never lets her hold his
green eyes for long.
Watching him
she thinks of watermelon
green and cool on a picnic table in the shade.
She remembers the sound
of a watermelon knocked off the table
falling on rocks
cracking open red
juice running out on the stones.
The tougher the rind
the sweeter the flesh
her grandma used to say
smiling.
She watches him arrogate the table
head high
tight denim on the planks
feet on the bench.
Her mouth waters.

Pat King
Albia, Iowa

Climate

A clank.
A pause.
The silent radiator,
like an old prison for snakes,
erupts in rebellious hisses
slithering the air in the room
along the temperature branch
from war to hot to stifling.

Reminding me of that night
I inched toward you, shedding clothes,
and you sidestepped away saying,
"It's too uncomfortable in here."
And I whispered, "I'll make you forget."
But you resisted the temptation
claiming it would be best to wait
for a more even atmosphere,

Which can not be. Because you prefer it cool.
And I never know how to turn the heat off.

Charles Fabrizio
New York, New York

Crosscountry

Careening west
slowing only when
through miles of rain
semis pass
blinding my view
as their giant wheels
and mudguards
hurl meanness at my windshield.

Never mind.
In checking pace
I notice drenched horses
huddled
in fields
forlorn.
It's so cold today.

When was it
I drove the long lane of
deep, dry, yellow leaves
(not a red among them)
watched wild geese
in their isotropic formations
steering smartly away from the cold
huddled
in their way
like the horses?

Then
the big rooms
the fire
it and I both
tranquil and nervous
fire, fire-eater
carrying too much sail
no ballast
mixing metaphors
oh the blame we can heap on drink.

Shall we lie like the coin silver in the drawer
spoon-fashion?
Shall this be the time?

Another voice
from another room
surging through hallways, stairs
filled all the spaces
swelled my mind
crowding out everything
everything
except
my fingers on eyelashes
moist
his voice trailing off unimportant explanation:
"I'm sorry, music does this to me . . ."

This poem is for
whoever put on
the Pavarotti.

Sarah P. Simmons
Washington, D.C. and Cedar Rapids, Iowa

Mind Control

Your hands,
rough and chapped
from working outdoors
grip my shoulders.

I raise my face
until my gaze meets yours.

There are no questions asked.
You drop your hands.
I turn and undress slowly,
knowing you are
lying in wait
upon the bed.

You reach and pull me
down to you.
I take one last breath
that I can call my own.
For now: I belong to no one
but you.

Renee Ingledue
State Center, Iowa

the light in my eyes is you
(for edie and a lifetime)

in latenight moments
of afterdinner afterglow
you audrey hepburn your way
into my fancies
        and i discover
        once more in the
        candled magic of
        your pixied aura
        that i want that
        h i d e a w a y
where we can wrap each other
in clovered comforters made
        of our love
and feel nightsights merge
into morningsongs
        on a screened porch
        of an enchanted bungalow
no one
    knows
        is there.

roger wilbur
Ellenwood, Georgia

Once Again

Your feminine body
Spoke to me sweetly
In the language of a kiss
Sensual sentences punctuated
The cold logic of my heart
Paragraphs of love
Descended upon the fort
Of my intellect
Once again you wrote
A composition of feeling
Which smote the seriousness
Of my abstractions

Mike Mihaljevich
Escondido, California

Night Visitor

The ground is covered with ice,
Sprinkled with diamonds that catch the sun.
The lawns in front of each house,
On our snow-covered street,
Are smooth and virginal as a frozen lake,
All except the house where the spinster,
Althea Abanathy, lives.
Across her lawn, right to her front door,
And back to the street again
The ice is torn and broken
By a double row of footprints
Made by the boots of a man who wears
About a size eleven.

Marie Grant
Jamesburg, New Jersey

The Sound of Boots

From that day in 1940,
I recorded in my memory
the sound of boots.
Germany invaded my homeland
of Amsterdam, Holland.

That night was my first time.
Anna and I were
in the act of copulation.
Men with guns broke down
the door and tramped up the stairs.

Fool! I thought, I would leave
the lamp burning downstairs!
Why don't they burn the house?
Anna and I would be bonded together.
The heat would weld us into one.

The soldiers uncoupled us.
They poked. They probed.
The spat on us.
That was my first
and last copulation.

Jack Bernier
Morongo Valley, California

Chapter 3

Pre-Boarding Call

Ominous as a long, grooved tongue
protruding
from a swollen throat, a stand

of stairs loomed
between me and my scheduled flight
on the screaming concourse.

With paramedic mastery
airline personnel strapped me in a stretcher-
chair and with laughter

chided me during the choppy
climb aboard.
I froze.

My hands cut the air like cold
propellers
sputtering,

but I trusted like a pilot
whose landing gear
had locked.

joan edwards
San Jose, California

Woman

Will I ride the circle 'round again, so late?
Coupled, will we brave this last, new journey?
My stomach scrambles; breasts and pelvis seem to round.
The scheduled secret sign is absent.

These sluggish days dim our recent, dear, happy genesis,
Making it seem distant, done-with.
I question the mirror's image of soft, asparkle eyes —
    inscrutable still —
How, so carelessly, could I have risked this woman?
Did her apparent invincibility charm me to forget
    to awe my woman's legacy?
Too freely embracing our pleasure, have I forever
    subdued her?

And, should there be another birth,
And she, consequently, die,
I wonder:
Could I bear her again?

Judith Lewis von Buchler
Anderson, Indiana

Shelf Life

White pickets are sprouting
along the perimeter
of the landscaped terrace,
surrounding the bungalow
nestled in the cul-de-sac.
Turning from the window,
the young woman wavers,
easing into the padded chair
to nurse her morning sickness.
Across the breakfast table
her husband is buried
in THE WALL STREET JOURNAL
while the reedy whisperings
of her silent flute
escape the sealed attic,
slipping down the hallway,
filling the kitchen
with the accompaniment
of unwritten melodies.
When her husband leaves,
the woodwind shrieks
and the music texts
vault from lofty places
on the library shelves,
unfurling their pages
against the rubber bumper
of her vacuum cleaner
as she dodges and feints,
steering across the floor.
Beyond the drawn drapes,
glinting in the sun,
the pickets are nudging
toward the limitless sky.

Jeff T. Dick
Davenport, Iowa

Visitor

Inside of me a babe
With big tits and
Red lips
Sits in full skirts
On hot cement steps,
Her legs spread wide.
She comes each day,
About the time your office opens,
And laughs at me
Washing dishes and ironing shirts.

When you come home,
She finishes her beer
And throws the crumpled can
On the floor across the room.
"You're no fun anymore," you say.
I turn to point,
But she has vanished,
Somewhere behind a playpen
Or under the washing machine,
Still waiting to be repaired.

Glenda Winders
Warrensburg, Missouri

HONORABLE MENTION

Rebirth

I shed you like a skin,
slip out of you a
second time.
You lie like a wrap.

You birthed me twice
and left me helpless.
Twice you slipped
the package off.

When you died I fought
to stay where it was warm.
I slid through that black
tunnel away from your
clear corpse like a big
girl.

I have not stopped
screaming yet.

Caroline St. Julien
Milwaukee, Wisconsin

Anxiety

From the first twitch in the womb,
anxiety holds on leech-like
to the heart
and burrows like a worm
into the dream.
It is an ugly twin to joy,
a pervasive spy
upon the privacy of love.
It crowds into the dominion of ecstasy
and can be measured
by never or forever
in the pressure of a kiss.
It frolics with the fool
and breathes down the neck of wisdom.
It crashes into calm.
With caprice, it rings a bell and warns —
persevere
or beats its drums incessantly
then mocks the vanquished victim.
It struggles like a beheaded serpent,
screaming in crescendos,
before it surrenders
to a valium
and sweet serenity
while the world rages on.

LaMoyne Nations
Joplin, Missouri

Slot Machine

I started out with silver dollars —
Feeding them into you:
Shiny, silver discs of hope
Into your bright, jangling jaws;
And you ate them greedily —
Spitting back one or two
Once in awhile
Just to prolong your feeding time.

Pretty soon it was halves, quarters —
If I keep on feeding you
Maybe you'll work for me.
But you're a grabbing, gobbling
Sonofabitch who takes —
Takes all I have, wants more
And tempts me every time I find a coin:
If I feed you just once more . . . .

It's nickels now — I'll give you my last one.
You'll eat that bright shining hope
And laugh at me — the hungry
Helpless one, whose pennies support
Your masters, taking all they can.
Broken — broke I stand before you,
Not a single coin for one more try —
Hopeless, in spite of what I know you hold.

You're a murdering bastard —
Why did they name you life?

J. M. Frank
Seattle, Washington

Sundays

when
i die
brains blown
in grey fury
against white walls

i will
know darkness
again as i did
when i lived
fetus-blind
in the womb

i will
lie quietly
upon a bed that
once groaned with
naked love

and all who
see me there
will know that
i am dead

when
the curious
ask, Why?

tell them

i died

to avoid
the pain
of stillborn
Sundays

Jill King
Florence, South Carolina

Proletarii

Like sterile hooded rats
they scurry frantically within
the brick-walled maze,
      Trapped
by the inescapable fact that
Yesterday is gone,
and has somehow been ill-used,
Whether through indifference
      or ignorance.
      (*advertere*)

In a grease-smeared kitchen
a mother sifts
through endless roaches to find
A bit of stale bread,
a dusty cracker,
      leftover,
To serve the wolf-eyed parasite
who screams, all stomach,
at her sleeve.
      (*cui bono?*)

She would cry, but tears
do not fill an empty belly.
She stares from the window
framing her life,
her silence her surrender.
In the sweaty night,
fumbling stickily, a well-oiled machine
spews more of her litter
on the treadmill to run
      (*revertere*)

Like sterile hooded rats
in a maze.

      (CAVEAT)

Laurre Breman
Indianola, Iowa

Poor Hygiene

The social worker has visited again
With complaints about my teenager at school —
About his strong barn smell and body odor —
And she sees the clutter and filth of my house,
But she has not known
The soft, quick breathing of my babies
And more than that she has not known
Our crowd of compassionate beings:
40 of them, gently shouting
Their misery and strength.
We feed them
Using tractors and pumps, conveyors,
And sheds, and fields.

— farm woman, 1983

Jeff Wright
Prairie du Chien, Wisconsin

Inconscient

With deceptive ease,
An insignificant sound
Or gesture
Can reveal to all of us
The witless absurdity
Of our complaisance.

Arthur C. Frick
Waverly, Iowa

Cobweb

I'm
caught
in the
cobweb
of life.
Tied tight
in the
sticky substance
of the spider's
thread.
The pattern
of passion
holds
me in
with its
regularity
and when I
struggle
and turn
the tighter and
tighter
it gets.

Frances R. Johnson
Hartland, Michigan

Preserving 17 Years of Marriage in a Savage Jungle

Divorce drums stir,
echo through suburbia
like tribal messages
pounded on stretched zebra hides.

After months of silence,
reassuring calm,
something fearful
once again stalks our neighborhood.

With quiet resignation,
you and I
watch victims fall,
comfort the stricken,
drink ourselves to oblivion
while we analyze
where they went wrong,
why we escaped again.

Dale Bryant
San Jose, California

The Mother Dreams

The mother dreams
Of sons and daughters
Making a go of it
But no war or accident
Because she worked so hard so long
    Her young daughter
    Wakes to forbidden thoughts
    And guilt and frustration
    As she searches for a release
    And that boy of hers
    That no one understands
    Drinks fermented dreams
    And looks for something to blame.
Her husband beside her wreckless sleep
Dreams of twenty and how did he end up
Sacrificing so his kids could hate
And his wife worry herself
To old age
    Next door
    Downtown
    The bum sleeps like a king
    Amid a flood of light
    On a newspaper
    Goose-down mattress
    The child sleeps deep
    And dreams of clowns and demons
    And sliding under
    The steps of an escalator

Brian Finney
St. Vincent, Minnesota

In the City

In the city, towers rise like
tall grass, like glass blades
turning edges to the sun.

In the city, geese come like
wild islands, cropping grass
in clouds of dandelion seeds.

In the city, seen from
swaying towers, clouds appear
as brooding wings.

Jim Albright
Bryan, Ohio

39th Street Elementary School

I'm scared to death to go to school!
I'm not a dependent
of a political official.
I don't have protection
from The White House,
FBI, CIA, or the NAACP.
There are snipers, Vietnam
Veterans, junkies, pushers,
pimps, police informants
out there walking this
jungle of playground courts.
Snipers shot three kids
last week, but the snipers
got away. You bet I am!
I'm scared to death to go to
the 39th Street Elementary School!

Jack Bernier
Morongo Valley, California

Confusion

Confusion . . .
It flows through me.
I don't know what to do,
where to go . . .
like an animal trying to escape a roaring fire,
like a painting with lines — colorful lines —
going everywhere, but having no meaing . . .
Confusion . . . it is . . .

Jennifer Dongvillo
Honor, Michigan
Age 10

Snow Storm

The time flies by.
It gusts like wizards.
Snow tumbles down
   and blows away.
Horses run and feet stamp
   like thunder,
throwing earth into the air.
They lay their ears back,
afraid of the snow storm.

Jennifer Riddle Cupples
Nantes, Quebec, Canada
Age 5

Waiting for Tigers

I remember being small
That I could sit behind the cedar hedge pretending forest.
And the patterned shade flickered like fire.

It was good to be waiting for tigers.
The days were warm and round and smooth in the coursing sun.
All I wanted then was to be grown and gone,
grown and gone.

Maxine Follstad
Pelican Lake, Wisconsin

Last Bus for Timbuktu

They run on shaky, spindly legs,
Hopping with jerky strides,
Frantically waving withered arms or wooden canes.
They croak a shout from age weakened voices.
Old people, the elderly, call them what you will,
Chasing the bus.
I wonder why?
It's not the last bus for Timbuktu.
I can hardly look at some of them
Boarding the bus.
Fragile, with panic in their eyes,
Five paces to a vacant seat,
An eternity of unbalanced, shuffling steps.
God! Their final reward for daring to grow old.
I have to look away,
I cannot bear to look into the eyes of my future.

Linda J. Reed
Minneapolis, Minnesota

The Turning Away

the road takes my
   bike with it,
only the wind
   fights this departure
from civilization:
it is a Southern Illinois autumn

I stop by a twisted metal fence
     that holds back the cows,
push my kickstand
     down:
hello how are you —
     no reply . . .
I am swayed by every car
      that races by
but the animals seem not to notice

some birds swoop and
     dart
above the cows,
     adding to the scene:

a calf lies in the grass
     while its mother hovers,
gently licks it:
   from the gravel roadside
I can see the big, pink, mother's
     tongue as it
     flip-flops
     back and forth
against the calf's back hide

  another calf
stands and stares at me
     then finally turns away,

unmoved:
   as dried leaves of corn
   turn away and move up,
   into the wind,
   imitating the birds:
   as I turn away from myself
   in this ride;

there is too much going on here,
       too much movement,
       too much life:
too much that I cannot be a part of

the plane overhead
   signals my return
   to the road
   to the incessant movement
   to rubber on asphalt
   to eye meeting tree
      meeting cornfield
and back again

like a car's windshield,
      my glasses are hit
by tiny insects
     as I ride

the sky is never the same:
     each time I look up it's
confused and
     seems ready to break open,
gushing forth uncertainties;
      it moves back and forth between
sun and gray,
  until it finally decides
  on a subtle mixture of the two

the land itself
wavers between green
    and golden:
the timothy hay,
    dry and tall,
overwhelms whatever
    green grass remains

I stop again,
  this time on a side road and,
perched on a mound of gravel
  overlooking a barren cornfield,
I see a leaf twitch in the sun
    and watch as a caterpillar slowly
  merges
and creeps along his own
    self-determined trail

. . . all things in flux
  all things turning away
    beating a path to their center,
      riding down a country road . . .

I return to my bike,
the wind,
the sun on my back,
and the slow, slow
  turning away
of the year into winter
and the self into self.

Margaret Brady
Chicago Heights, Illinois

FIRST PLACE POEM

The Drowning
(to the novelist, Virginia Woolf)

You knew where you were going
when you gathered coat and walking stick
and went, without a word, through the garden gate,
on out toward the water meadows.

What did you choose a morning,
a late morning,
when no early mist
could shroud your lonely walk
down to the river,
stooping, like a child,
gathering stones
to fill your jacket pockets?

Who, seeing you, could have known
those stones would hold you low, low,
until the water collapsed
in a deeper current?

The sun, if it could have born to shine,
must have struck the water
like a sword
until the day it finally gave you up.

(Now the river calmly rocks and runs
that closed, welcome, over your elegant head.)

But some part of you,
stronger than anguish,
refused the drowning,
struggled out.
Did you remember
that in your paper-strewn study at Monks House
you had left your only valid passport
to life?

There, under the elms
beside the low wall of the garden
that looks out over the water meadows,
the one who loved you most
has set a simple stone
carved with your own words,
knowing you would need to come back home.

Martha K. Graham
Macomb, Illinois

FOURTH PLACE POEM

Mother's Nursing Home Roommate

She arrived like a breath of fresh pine needles
the day after Christmas
and immediately gave the room
a feeling of coming to life
as she began crocheting an afghan.
The Indian design of tan
was that of an ancient medicine man
in modern drug society —
weaving tan trails of yarn
interspersed with red beaded pills
like the ones they use
to charm her cancer.

Jerri Evans
Cherokee, Iowa

Grief

Danny was an Iowa boy
With hands as hard as horn.
He walked with the gait of the rolling plains
Tall and straight as corn.
And I loved Danny dearly
And he loved me like sin.
Our little house held dreams
And rest and joy within.
But Danny was a proud Marine.
They shipped him over the sea —
To help keep peace in Lebanon —
With all his Company.
He was the man on guard that night
The bombs fell like rain.
"They shot him down! They shot him down!"
And he'll never come home again.
They sent me a fancy letter
And a medal all engraved
"Above and beyond his duty
Fifty lives were saved."
But what are fifty men to me
Nights long in my bed.
What are fifty men alive
With young Dan dead.
And who will ever name our sons,
The young men never born
To walk with the gait of the rolling plains
Tall and straight as corn.

Enid M. Bennett
Keokuk, Iowa

John

John played football in high school
was all-state
but not enough to get a scholarship
anyway
scholastically he fell short of college
his parents told him they
were disappointed.
he could care less for awhile
but then it got to him.
he went off to fight in Nam
said that he had something
to prove to himself, his parents,
his country.
fought with the infantry
called him a "swamp rat"
10 months in combat
and then it ended
John never came home
his parents moved away
forgetting memories behind
and John lies still
with nothing left to prove
anymore.

Virgil Chabre
Rock Springs, Wyoming

Worlds Apart

The first thing I noticed
about Jack was his eyes.
Oh, the face was the same,
but the eyes that had seemed
to radiate warmth
had gone hollow.
Still, we talked.

I talked of stock deals,
of car payments and rent control
and jock itch.
He talked of bombs,
of flying over ruined villages
watching people die,
and of emptiness inside.

He spoke with pain,
I listened and felt the same pain,
pain of things seen that shouldn't exist,
pain that forced us to shut things out,
pain that made him go numb inside
just so he could cope.

I knew nothing I could say
could cover the distance,
the miles that separated our realities —
the one I wouldn't face and
the one he couldn't come back to.
So we sat and stirred our drinks,
two very different relics
of the same strange times.

Ron MacLean
Monterey Park, California

Chapter 4

The Old Men

Now that I am fifty
I say gray
Damn the old men!

Who run our lives
And tangle us with love
For wars they remember
But did not die in
Who think that to live
Is to dare young death.

Damn the old men
For their callousness
Toward the tender poor
Fat old men with food
Who frank their letters
And pay for cars with cash

The old men
With gentle courtesy
And hinged hats
Old men building pedestals
For their women
Decorated toys

Pale old men
With pink skin
Blessed by god
With power
and racial purity

Damn the old men!
Pissing in the river
Coughing acid smoke
Stripping earth bare

Buying young men
To take their places
With promotions
And executive keys
Promises that they
Will be old
Before their time

Damn the young men!
Who want to be old

Now I am fifty
And want to live
Without war
Warm and easy
In our equity

Build something beautiful
Take dancing lessons
And drink red wine.

Conrad Simonson
Decorah, Iowa

In God's Image

I am not ready to let him go,
So do not talk to me of peace
and heavenly reward.
He is my son and I will feel no
relief if he goes.
God wanted his son back.
I am no different than God.

Ann J. Majure
Red Oak, Iowa

Anger

Anger is a fireball
screaming through the sky,
destined to reach its target
unless
peace can prevail
and quench the fires of anger
with its ocean blue mist.

Michael Felsburg
Honor, Michigan
Age 11

Mistakes

We build atomic plants
in barrios, in ghettos
    and in reservations
we bleach ugly graffiti
— the handwritings on the walls
that we do not see
scrawlings on dusty circuituous roads
that lead where they began.

We the gifted
we the judge
we the warden
    of them who have nothing
    they who are nothing
just by luck
    presently.
But when our robotics security
    springs a leak
who has everything to lose?

Chema Ude
Riverside, California

Solomon On High

*(Kenya Open Tennis Tournament
Nairobi Club, February, 1983)*

British dignity's in place,
with umpire's power perched
beneath the scorching sun.

Mad dogs make war across the net;
they curse, complain
and claim consistent persecution
by that arbiter of law upon the court

He cannot favour those who play like gentlemen,
or be bullied by the egos of the net.
He calls Advantage where it's due,
and shouts out Love
without emotion.

*Mike Eldon
Nairobi, Kenya, Africa*

The Minstrel

I shall sing of the glories of nature,
   Drink a toast to the birds, and the bees,
I shall sing of the flowers,
     of warm summer showers,
  The sun, and the breeze, and the trees.

And while I am singing of nature,
   The snow, and the wind, and the rain,
Volcanos are spewing, and hurricanes brewing,
Tornados are growing, and fires are glowing,
And earthquakes are splitting,
     and tidal waves spitting,
And termites are eating,
     and deserts are heating,
And rivers are drying, and animals dying,
And storm clouds come scudding,
     and pastures are flooding,
  And mildew is ruining the grain.

BUT, I'll sing of the glories of nature,
   And lament all the follies of man,
OK, I shall sing; for the hell of the thing,
   And I'll keep a straight face. If I can.

June L. Shipley
Highland, Indiana

To Stephen King

So, you think you can scare me
with tales of
ignitable teens,
murderous cars and
pets becoming rabid
or worse,
resurrected.
Well, you have.
I no longer
chaperone teen dances,
will avoid
Plymouth Furies,
and never
travel through Maine.
(by the way,
has their Tourist Bureau
complained to you?)
Stephen King,
if you set your next novel
in Kansas,
I'm sunk.

Marie Asner
Shawnee, Kansas

Poet's Prayer To His Muse
(With Apologies)

Haste Thee, Nymph, and bring with thee
    Status and fame — publicity!
A check ye creditors to beguile —
That wanton nod that bring a smile
    to lip, to brow, to cheek, to eye —
Then, prythee, darling — stay a while.
Of progeny may we beget
    A sonnet and a triolet.

Let not the fledgling verse depart
Too far from doting parent's heart:
Ne'er to the void may it descend:
    A basket-case ne'er be its end.
Nay! Be it touted far! Imprinted wide!
    So I in cozy comfort bide!

E. Wright
Port Huron, Michigan

A Complaint Addressed to W.B. Yeats

You, Willie Yeats, can lie in your graveled grave
and grin, while we must fight for every line —
granted, as you did once, that dying confounds
the critics, at least for a while; they must assess
and reassess, must build their elegant structures
and cannot ask: "But here, what did you mean?"

But we, the living, are not so lucky, Willie.
Our critics badger us: "What does this mean?"
"Why this, not this?" "How do you justify
this choice?" "What *is* your poem, anyway?"
My poem is what I am, my art and craft
Please, Willie, help me; they think my verses daft!

Will C. Jumper
Ames, Iowa

Anguish and Ecstacy

I have no titles for the poems drawn
Like festering splinters from the edge of being,
No muscles that can emulate the brawn
My spirit needs for breaking bonds, and freeing
My thoughts to grow in sun that nourishes
Each budding tendril to a strength that stands
Alone and proud — a plant that flourishes
Without the nurturing of parent hands.
I have no titles and perhaps few words
To shape clear pictures of the colors massed
On my horizons, outline soaring birds
That fly through now out of a clouded past.
I only have the bent and battered will,
The vast horizons and unpeopled hill.

Alice Mackenzie Swaim
Harrisburg, Pennsylvania

Ann Sexton

died in October, 1974. I
had just had surgery,
carrying a bag of Ann's books
with me to the hospital.
Oh Ann! Ann!
Forbidden to drive for a month
I walked to the Guidance Center,
volunteering as Ann did with children,
changing my own bandages and
finding the gauze and tape expensive,
sleeping in a rented hospital bed
at home in the room where
my father died.
Oh Ann! Ann!
Ann Sexton is out of style.
Suicide is out of style.
I was glad to be alive
and writing poetry.

Linda Curtis
Urbandale, Iowa

The Survivor

It was a terrible accident, they said.
The taxi, screaming like a beast of prey,
   triumphant, crushed me to the earth.
I'm lucky to be alive, they said.

Insignificant words, all meaningless.
Just let me be.
Let me slip into my own insanity,
   and wallow through black memories,

> (. . . men like cattle in great numbers drilled
> in human flesh streaked livid and red-tinged
> smoke from sullen stacks of men, women and
> children ravished by men. . .)

Down, down to a darker spot.
There.
A burning secretly revered:
   the image of that speeding cab,
   my own hands upon the wheel.

Laurre Breman
Indianola, Iowa

Cat-Scan

these terrible enigmas
that constitute our prison
darkness of the unprocessed wood
& the unbuilt flame
the gold that lingers in the eye
after it has been shut
I hear the frame of the ambulance
as it crosses the bridge
the river is a strip
of tin dull and unreflecting
the city of the world
which we enter as through a tunnel
shudders and its houses and tenements
are the very models of distance
they show us into the hospital
through the back way
a cavern of modern rugs
and electrical apparatus
the new form of x-ray machine
which will show the mind
sectioned by light from the other world
of one of angels
whose erect personae
represent the letters of hell
dim flares reveal thoughts in decay
the intention to rest
sleep ominous and omnipresent the blood
runs the other way
the tooth fixes on its own shadow
                                          like marble
the will does not yield

Ivan Argüelles
Berkeley, California

In The Meantime

Those who get help from Chemotherapy
and are currently in remission,
walk cautiously,
as if asking permission,
with backward glances
and ears to the ground
to catch the drum beat sound
and hear the mighty roar
of the enemy, as before.
Fearful, yet daring to hope
for a new discovery
and a full recovery.
Waking up to each new day
thankful, yet wondering,
"Why this stay?"
Please delay
   The Thing
      for awhile.

Esther Edleman
Lost Nation, Iowa

Last Years

Now, when winter comes
And I could warm myself
By the open fire,
I find no chair in which to sit,
No friends with whom to chat
And only grey ashes on a cold hearth.

Frances H. Hughes
Danville, Illinois

Midgard

There is a heaven
and as many different hells
as we care to create.

I walk somewhere between,
or maybe all my childish
Our Fathers and Hail Marys
have paid off.

My mind has become
the purgatory of
my life.
I know no heaven
nor have I met any
demons lately.

I stopped praying
a long time ago.
Not even a good
Act of Contrition
recently.

I watch. I wait.
I dread the day
I'll have to decide
what position to take.
Maybe someone else
will decide for me.

If that day must come,
please, God, don't
let it be today.

Ronald L. Andrzejewski
Kentwood, Michigan

Winter Comes

I

The sky's on fire
Forever tonight:
Glowing coals
Rapidly cooling
To mounds
Of white-gray ash.
The sun is gone —
It will snow soon.

Half-moon lights
Gray, swollen,
Heavy clouds —
Smoky visions:
Somnolent hearth,
Lover's arms,
Mulled wine —
A season to drema in.

My house is empty.
Hollow waiting,
Ringing silence,
Echoing cold,
I don't want winter —
Oh, God — not alone,
Not alone this time:
I don't want winter!

II

The Great white silence —
I could feel it
Before I opened the drapes.
Fearing its loneliness
I had forgotten its peace.

The ashes have fallen —
I knew they would,
And dreaded the moment.
I had forgotten the joy
Of a dying sky.

J. M. Frank
Seattle, Washington

Picasso

the hairy
bull of passion
manly art of which
you are a part,
and guilt
of which
will
is at the heart.
The beast of love
is only a match
for the
wish
of the dove
who flutters and
flutters in her white
in the night
as the
cape and sequins
entices the
charge.

Frances R. Johnson
Hartland, Michigan

Long Abandoned, Yet Still It Stands

Long abandoned
Yet it stands
Crooked timbers shrinking from the wind
Rotting wood, broken windows
A shell with sightless eyes
Yet still it stands

Memories linger within those walls
Long days of work
Homesteading, family-raising
Births and deaths
Sons in uniform, daughters altar bound

Then two old people
Sitting at the kitchen table
Drinking coffee
Looking out the window
At fields going to seed

Finally, nothing left
Except the memories
And the wooden frame

Long abandoned
Yet still it stands

Sheryl Carlon
Virginia, Minnesota

The Chestnut Tree

Torso endures, enormous
blighted, roots erupting. One
hugh & gnarled socket
hoards two centuries. One
bronzed plaque

announces
its extinction
against the living forest. Sixty years
without spring to electrify
its greyness. Amputated
branches
give astonished benediction
midpoint on this country road
between a life-long friendship. One
kilometer south, Mrs. Alberta Moses & her wooded
cottage nestle. One mile north
Miss Katherine Woolsey Goodenough and her gaunt farm
set firmly in the fields. They drive past
this lifeless landmark Wednesdays
slowly on their way
to market. Ease crackling bodies
in & out of Bertie's old green Plymouth. Phone
each other three times daily. Bertie's
rounded brownness sings; her laughter splits
the air like geese
envelopes wounded branches. Katherine's
fingers, parsnip-pale
flutter blue & coiled ringlets; they seem
to hold her spine straight, keep her
starched into her chair. Her trembling mouth
becomes a smile. Coughing she speaks
gently: I trust your legs are better, Alberta. Her
awkwardness, kind as magic, thunders
down the lines. Bertie brushes off
her lilaced apron. Her eyes glow
warm as spices: Kate, dear, you drink
lots of tea and honey, hear. Moonlight
shimmer up & down the wires
falling on the tree like flowers.

Sherrill Morgan Finn
New Hartford, Connecticut

Staigue Fort, Ireland

Old it is,
built when folk were new
and the hills ringing them round
already ancient.
On its gentle rise
sheep gaze now within the perfect circle,
while all around
the Kerry mountains rise up,
another fortress, more primitive,
more foreboding than ever human hand could make.
Bracken gone red in the winter's dying
trickles like blood down the bared rock,
flayed by the salt wind keening in from the sea.
So old, so old. . . .
The dust of those ancient, frightened folk
is the soil of this place,
the heart of it;
living in savagery and splendor,
they were new, untried,
in a world already old and hard.

Stand at the top of the fort,
lift your face to the mountains and sky,
and see through their eyes the wonder,
the deep mysteries, the striving required.
See the concentric circles, widening ever,
from fort to mountains to the Ring of Kerry,
beyond, infinitely, and back.
Millenia after this fort's abandonment
new folk arrive, curious, awed,
half-aware of older, deeper mysteries:
In the West of Ireland, lost in a different time,
the ring fort, the mountains, the sea,
the folk endure
as they always shall.

Ann Caroline Kabel
Obernburg am Main, West Germany

HONORABLE MENTION

To Sacajawea at Riverton

(A larger-than-life bronze of Sacajawea and her infant son Baptiste by world renowned sculptor Harry Jackson stands at the south entrance to Central Wyoming College at Riverton, Wyoming.)

Bronzed woman,
Baptiste enfolded in your blanket robe,
beautiful in full moonlight
forever leading the white man west,
do you sometimes, in the dark of the moon,
turn south on your Harry Jackson pedestal
opening your arms to your people?
Do you think of long forgotten braves
and the hunting grounds now reservation?
Do you weep for the wrong done Washakie?
And when you turn back west,
do you sigh for Shoshoni women
gathering berries along the Sisk-ke-dee?
Or do you sometimes turn north
to the symbol of learning beside you
hoping for enlightenment among people?
Do you sometimes, just before dawn, face east
turning to God born at Bethlehem
coming again to right all wrongs?
In sunlight, I see thee
always windswept, always westward.

Kay Jons Roelfsema
Steamboat Rock, Iowa

Chapter 5

Love Song for My Native State

Iowa is the cellar of my life-home, my
retreat when it gets too hot in my kitchen,
the deliciously cool, apple-fragrant refuge
to which I glide on the escalator of memory.

When other loves forsake me, one Love stays
And she is beautiful beyond my power
To tell; she is a place — a State — whose praise
I ever sing, where crops and genius flower
To stock the world. No frilly gown she wears
But deep black soil with scarf of summer greens
Or winter white; her jewels she freely shares
(Her suitors' sustenance) — her corn, her beans,
Her melons, apples, grapes. O, yes, my Love,
I have been long away, but watch for me
When scarlet oaks and maples flame above
Your browning plains, when pheasants stealthily
Glean frosty fields where hungry cattle roam —
When winter nears, I will be coming home!

Joan Merryman Burns
Griffin, Georgia

Plains Summer

Nestled in the cool eaves
above my window,
a frocked dove soothes,
cooing its avian hymn.

Out across the plains
dressed in its estival best,
grey-hooded lizards lisp
under thirsty succulents
and blink, blocking
the restless sun's raze.

While on the stoop below,
a chubby brown toad squats —
still, wrinkled sphinx.
Its freckled throat
expands, contracts,
tic toc, tic, toc.

Such a shallow-breathed, waiting
moment
is August, easily.

Eleanor Mader
College Station, Texas

HONORABLE MENTION

Bathroom Alien

Little orange mushroom
clinging to a sterile
black and white
checkerboard plain.
Borne inside:
Lodged in the dust of a gritty crevice.
No inching upward
on a spongy leaf mold bed
surrounded by your own kind:
Isolated here!
I kneel down to discuss with you
the possibility of a transplant:
"Have you the heart for it?"

Doris T. Brokaw
Canton, Missouri

Garden Follies

No matter how much
Love and care
I give to yellow roses,
They poke their petals
Through the fence
And my neighbor thinks she grows them.

Mildred Hope Wood
Cedar Falls, Iowa

Imprints

On my walk today
I stepped in snow
where no person
had gone before

I traced prints of deer
rabbit and pheasant
but none of humankind
the air was cold
wind strong
my steps slow
and I was lonely

until I came upon two students
changing a back tire
gone flat

today I needed
that piece of world
more than beauty

Clo Weirich
Sioux City, Iowa

Pre-Dawn Vigil

The sky is at the north —
A moon stares — wafer-round —
Day old snow gleams —
I wait
forever — for a sound . . . .

Myrtle T. Cavallo
Danbury, Connecticut

Identity

It's a warm January thaw day
I observe the new curtains I have made
and the way my walls look
in this old house that feels like home.

I am the kind of person
that expresses self in surroundings
I center myself in the wood
of my table, and cut of the cloth.

I feel best in familiar sights
my old ceramic cup suits me best
plants that have weathered my years
mean the most.

I can see myself here
years from now, bringing in flowers
from the garden, putting them in
a mason jar on my oak table.

Having a cup of coffee, reading
a good book, satisfied,
not caring that I am old
having my life visible around me.

Jean Marie Schultz
Stillwater, Minnesota

The Peach Tree Blooms

How can you
in the numb,
white earth-places
know how I feel (now)
where the sun
has drawn
the green blade
and unsheathed
the fuzzy, brown
of the peach tree
buds?

My spring feet
dig deeply
into the brown
hope of harvest
as I plant.

I look
at my long past
and wonder
what I have planted
for those
who come after
me.

Later
I will ride
the white sky
into your cold
while you sleep
like the crocus
and dream
of the sun
while my peach tree
blooms.

Iva Nelle Simak
Fennimore, Wisconsin

Remembrance

Whenever
  I plant
    canna bulbs in the Spring . . .
I think of my Dad
(Perhaps
  that's
    why
      I
        plant
          them)
And later when they bloom,
I remember his (and him)
Standing brave and tall and colorful
In the corner
    Of our yard.

Jean Lollich Warner
Clinton, Iowa

My Mother

She comes to me again
when wild white violets bloom,
bending her regal braided head
to sniff their faint perfume.
She comforts me then.

Esther Edleman
Lost Nation, Iowa

For Papa, The Last Time

Winter in Pennsylvania
and the road home
pulls like a tendon;
aches when it stops.

My hand is a shadow
against yours.
You grip it.

For an instant
you shelter me again,
like a tree without leaves.

Private mountains
move inside you,
named, but left unsaid.

Death shadows the branches
like snow, as I drive back
to Illinois.

One last flock of geese
ravels into the sky,
flickers at the treeline,
leaves me with this poem.

Lynne Proctor Sancken
Tolono, Illinois

Growing Sweetcorn

Early spring, the dirt
warms under my nails,
listening as the kernels become
a secret we share.

As I weed, the sun
slows my fingers, stained
with buttonweed. My knees grow tough
as these little plants.

Soon, you burst fountains,
become a thick tide.
I stand below. You outreach me,
stop, and tassle out.

Your ripe husks open
green lips revealing
their rows of even teeth that smile
as they nourish me.

Lynne Proctor Sancken
Tolono, Illinois

Evening Sonnet

(for Tatiana)

When evening hangs its deeper shades of gray
Upon the row of rustling poplar trees
That stands outside my window, then I may
Be moved by whim to wander as I please.
Amid the tall and softly chanting grass
That grows along the lake, I sometimes see
At such an hour a startled blackbird toss
Himself aloft on scarlet wings to flee.
At my approach, he acts just like the fool
I used to be, when from your gentle touch
I'd run in haste and fear. It was my rule
To guard my heart and never love too much.
Now like the chanting grass, I ever sing
A song of thanks for my awakening.

Michael Gfoeller
Fremont, Ohio

To Dale

Like gentle summer rain
Your love has seeped
Into my deepest being
Where, having been stored
These several years,
From a sweet underground well
It rises again to the surface
To overflow in love
To those whose lives I touch.

Meg Kramer
Truman, Minnesota

Caring

A man, a woman
forever caring,
needs and desires
together sharing,
hopes and dreams
in fearless daring,
unto each other
their hearts baring.

With love so true
they give unsparing,
a gift of life
beyond comparing,
in pride and joy
so bright and glaring,
the woman now
a child is bearing.

Until, at last,
in wonder staring,
at what was wrought
through time and caring,
needs and desires
in passions pairing,
with hopes and dreams
and loves declaring.

A newborn child
its life-force flaring,
unto the world
its challenge airing,
to grow in strength
and freedom, wearing
love and truth
with regal bearing.

A man, a woman
once declaring,
they would all others
be foreswearing,
are now their love
with their child sharing;
a man, a woman
forver caring.

R. J. Caylor
Jacksonville, Florida

Certainty

My confidence in
your love is as certain as
tomorrow's sunshine.

Catherine Boulanger
Highland, Illinois

Benevolence

We are but one
    in a multitude of many
forever caring, forever sharing
    the undying love
we have between us.

Aaron Koch
Carlisle, Iowa
Age 15

Something Blue

I'll not be wearing grandmother's lace today,
but I will carry her stubborn streak that stood
at the gate and shooed an outlaw on his way,
set the rifle down, and chopped more wood;
quoting, ". . . the Lord giveth and . . . taketh away."

Grandfather will be my something new to wear;
he likes change, says it's better than old ways,
not just for the sake of change, but as to dare
to stretch beyond the safe yesterdays.
Something old, something new, what will borrowed spare?

I'll borrow the back of my grandmother's pride,
a back unbent and a head held high;
and the giving and love she could never hide
like the sad she hides that wants to cry
because it's a wedding, because I'm the bride.

My grandfather twinkles, my grandmother prays,
and quite suddenly I'm what is blue.
If my stubborn streak and my pride bend both ways,
and I am scared to death of what's new —
will I sniffle or smile at pledging, 'obeys'?

Dorothy J. Turnour
Ontario, California

We're All Parents Now

lately i look back at free feeling
                    fast reeling
                    cartwheeling
days of our youth
shake my head in astonishment
we're all parents now
oh, we've gained and lost so much

remember how the back of a motorcycle
did the trick
supplied the kick
we were so slick to
surround ourselves with leather and chrome
                    free to roam
we used the rumbling V- Twin like a salve

now our rides are more sedate
V- Twins are generally V- 8
the molded frames
   metallic flames
that licked our sides like hounds of hell
forever urging faster, faster
                  it was a gas, yeah
                  now all past

did we ride the Glory Road
is it just some story someone told
me late late one long summer night
sitting by the glow of a bunny lite
as the dog rolls on the grass outside
we remember what it's like to ride
you stroke my hair
i nurse the babe . . .

we're all parents now

Noni Bookbinder Bell
Vincentown, New Jersey

Mother's Song to Newborn

The presence of your warm and dreaming life
Spreads through me awake, asleep, my thoughts
Like the slow stir of water through bedrock.

Your heart-race is still tied to mine.
The pace of your breathing winds me round and round
By fragile strings that pull and sing, that cry my freedom
The space I might have had alone.

You are a love-stone,
A begging flower.
Your tight hands fist the fibers of my nature so that
Hour by hour I am drawn down, drawn out
By your power.

Maxine Follstad
Pelican Lake, Wisconsin

Dreams

Let not morning sun
Caress your brow
Nor moonlight stroke your cheek
Until I've shared my love so you
Can dream it in your sleep

Mary Pagliaro
Verona, Wisconsin

Someday, My Little One

Someday, my little one,
when you're a little older,
someday, I'll tell you all about
these most beautiful of days.
We'll bow our heads together
over the snapshot book,
and I'll bring back from memory
the wonder of your ways.
How your sweet, soft voice
caused excitement with each word,
how your happy smile,
when you called my name,
made it the best I've ever heard.
Your toddling steps
were a source of joy
I never tired of seeing.
When your little hand
reached up to mine,
I thanked God for your being.
I'll tell you all about it,
someday, my little one.

Kay Logsdon Pearce
O'Fallon, Illinois

Walk

We walk to the playground,
your tiny hand stretched upward to meet mine,
and your feet taking two steps to my every one.
The spring air sends wisps of wind
through your wavy locks of golden hair.
And I see that a smile is fixed upon your face,
as you busily chatter away about the wonders of the outdoors.
Rocks, leaves, bushes, flowers, trees; they all
enthrall you. You squeal.

Communication flows as you relay your delight to me,
it's in your words. It is spread across your face,
it is captured in the way
you jog along.
I watch you run
up ahead of me,
pondering how you have grown
and all that you have mastered
in two short years.
You came to me a tiny, dependant being
and here you are now,
skipping along the sidewalk on this breezy
spring afternoon.

You have taught me something important today.
I feel the simple joy of this outdoor jaunt.
It was a pleasure once known, that I'd long ago forgotten.
Now, I too, am enthralled.

Mary Himka Young
Wixom, Michigan

I'll Miss You

O Meghan, I'll miss you:
   the uninhibited way
   you laugh and hug
   when you climb up
   on my lap for a story;
   your soft cheek against
   mine as you drowse upon
   my shoulder;
   the exuberance displayed
   at discovering ants;
   your delight in each new day.
In a few years I will dote on
   your expanded inventiveness,
   newly-acquired composure
   and self-consciousness,
But I'll definitely miss
   this two-year-old
   version of you.

Margery Disburg
Marshalltown, Iowa

In the Little House

on East 23rd Street South,
the kids, so small
all four could fit in one bed,
would fall asleep
early in the evening.
The women would be visiting
in the brightly lighted kitchen,
while in the dimly quiet livingroom,
you and I, my friend,
drank our wide mouth barrels
of Blatz beer
and discussed the world's
most important topics.
Later, Seals and Crofts would sing "Oh, Hummingbird"
on your record player
and the women would join us then
to listen.

William P. Riddle
Colfax, Iowa

Mother's Day — 1984

During a desiring May
  (it was a super day),
We roasted things on a boasting fire
  with sticks
    carved from wood.
Water drippled down a creek;
  a baby cried;
    the water was such a beautiful sight.

Rocks moving;
  creekweed growing;
such it was,
  a beautiful sight.

A very nice mom
  making us ice cream;
    birds chirping,
      on that beautiful Mother's Day.

Justin Mitchell Sytsma
Des Moines, Iowa
Age 9

Rocking Chair Frame

imagined shore
plants
log cabin.
        slippers
        slap
        sole sound.
                calico fur
                curls into
                motes
                mellow.

star
morning guide to
sky light cathedral.
        cardinal
        soars
        on clear note.
                hands-in-pocket
                walk
                reflective.

birds
chirp
picnic remembrances
creek style.
        bittersweet
        tied
        with thin lavender
        ribbon.
                lullabies
                hum
                untasted
                grandchildren.

daily
companion
woman, seventy
child, seven.

Sharon L. Buettell
Dubuque, Iowa

Dad and Dominoes

He crossed his legs at the knee;
his foot dangled.
The black and white tile
he held was dwarfed by the
size of his large, weathered hand.

"I hate this game, I can't
add fast enough!"

He reached for the boneyard,
drew several more tiles before
he could play.
Every time he cursed.

"Finally! Can I put the double
nine here?"

His big clumsy hand laid the tile
sideways in a pattern of strange
looking dimensions before him.

He watched as his opponent thought
and played a scoring tile,
forcing him to labor again over
his next play.

On and on this went.
He had one tile left.

"Don't mess up my play."

She didn't.

He quickly placed his last tile
in the maze on the table.
His eyes twinkled.

"Count your spots.
Another game, dear?"

Marsha A. Mitchell
Centerville, Iowa

The Physics of Ten

Street water lures
the child of ten
   in a coat bulging with down,
      when it's frozen to careen,
      risking equilibrium,
   with jacket undone, hat pocketed
      when it's mush to track,
      imprinting zig-zag treads;
   with windbreaker off and trailing an arm
      when it's liquid to splash
      in knee-high steps.

In the physics of ten
dry concrete repels
but water in any season lures
the child to go
on,
   into,
      through
it on the street.
the child has water,
slick,
   slush,
      or puddle,
as Einstein had space and stars
   to play with

Jean Kennedy
Waterloo, Iowa

Horseshoe Luck
(For Laura, an Iowa Child)

My daughter shows me a horseshoe
she has found and nailed on wood.
I turn it in her hand, explaining
the ends are up to hold in the luck
I tell her my mother chuckled at the unknowing
who hung horseshoes with luck falling out.

My daughter is at the age for luck pieces,
tokens to trade for what she wants but sees
no way to get by her own doing.
Yet all her bright hopes rest on the work
of those who claimed this virgin sod
and by horses reined and furrows turned
broke from the prairie the golden spill
of grain, town streets, and city avenues.
Fields they plowed are paved and platted now,
yet sometimes a token from the past turns up.

"It wasn't horsehoe luck that harnessed
horse to plow at dawn," I say aloud.
"Reaping follows sowing sure as the seasons turn."
But she with the hope of a bursting seedling
has run to her room to hang the horseshoe cupped.

Jean Kennedy
Waterloo, Iowa

On Giving a Saint Christopher Medal

I give this token to you
because the child in me
wants to shield you
with my own flesh if need be
from pain
for your journey home
and for all your life
although the mother knows
you could never have grown
to the man you are
without your share of tears
and although the woman knows
this business of Saint Christopher
is just a bit of whimsy
by which I can say
what I may not say
or even feel:
would God I were Saint Christopher
to ride on a silver chain
and touch you
and feel your heart beat
all your life.

Pat King
Albia, Iowa

When My Daughter Visits

She comes bringing brilliance
too bright for draped rooms,
too hot for snow covered hills.
The perfume of her youth
so stirring it hurts.
Her impatience and vitality
alarming to my staidness.
A whirlwind blowing
sweet grit of the past
into my eyes, blurring
away all but love.
Whirling about for days;
whirling away leaving
a pale world
that gradually
takes on the hues
of acceptance.

Delores Mundell
New London, Missouri

HONORABLE MENTION

Twins

Two rivers,
   my life and yours.
A confluence
   rolling together in unison.
No apprehension, no tension . . .
   symmetry, sweet harmony.

The water divides;
   not into the same two rivers.
Each has become a part of the other.

You are my twin, my mate, my brother.
May the caress of the wind
   and the lure of the moon
   remind you of me.

And two shall again be one.

Ann Switzer Walters
Gibson City, Illinois

To You, Away

I hear faint, faint whispers
Of your music . . .
I feel faint ripples
Of your song.
Those dreams, quietly,
    Softly,
        Descending on your memory . . .

Faint yesterdays
    Sing your tunes and
Soft tomorrows, now open,
    Await your
Coming.
    Sweet yesterdays
        Recall rhythmic ecstacies . . .
            Ripples of your song.

Minneh M. Karanja
Nairobi, Kenya, Africa

The Fun House

You always loved the Fair.
The Fun House was your favorite.
You'd stand for hours
Posing in front of the mirrors
Delighting as your body
Changed shape and size

The way your face stretched
Into forms you couldn't duplicate
In your silliest moments.

I watched you
In the silvered glass
And was secretly pleased
That your arms looked long enough
To wrap around me
Twice.

Linda Lee Curtis
Phoenix, Arizona

Inheritance

My nephew is part English,
And Scotch, we all agree
His grandmother is Kosher Jew
As sweet as she can be.

When I said the best of two worlds
Had he, he countered quietly,
"Will you explain to my grandmother
The need for a Christmas tree?"

Mary Hamilton Neary
Wichita, Kansas

Thanks for My Unfriend

Margaret doesn't like me much,
hardly at all. But Margaret does
love Jesus Christ. When Margaret speaks
to me with love she really speaks
with Christ's love. She can give
to me a better gift than friends
who really like me as I am.
Thank you, God, for Margaret.

Corinne B. Ansell
Klamath Falls, Oregon

Damned If You Do

i proceeded to follow
my therapist's advice
and learned to love myself
twice as nice
but there must have been
something that i missed
because now everyone thinks
i'm an egotist.

Dean M. LeBel
St. Louis, Missouri

Three Traditional Kabyle Songs

Love Song
(Fountain Spy Song)

I found her standing near the fountain,
Waiting her turn in the oak tree's shade.
Her skin as pure as milk
Is liken only to
The budding dawn.
When I called out, she turned around,
I felt then that she knew me.
Bent over like a lovely reed, she smiled at me.

Am I Forgotten
(Dance Song)

Flowering Oleander
Which thrives in the shade,
Do ask the young man
If I am forgotten.

Towering date-palm
Be covered with fruit!
And tell me — that young man —
Has he started out?

Fruitladen mulberry
Let my heart forget him!
But ask my beloved,
If he's coming back.

A Girl Abandoned on the Day of Her Wedding
(A Round)

My mother, O my mother,
Here I am all dressed up
And no one came to claim me.

My daughter, O my daughter,
Did they come?
Did I refuse them?

I'm all ready
But now I am scorned.

Did they present themselves?
Did I run off?

You must help me.
I've put on my most beautiful things
And I stayed.
And the curious came
And they laughed at me.

You must pray to God
That a young man will come
And he will dream of you.

I've already prayed to God
But an old man came,
Not a handsome young lad.

Don't marry him!
Old men's marriages
Smell like toads.
But young lad's marriages
Have the scent of fresh butter.

Translated from the Berber language into French by Marguerite Taos-Amrouche, and retranslated into English by Charlotte H. Bruner, Ames, Iowa

Deer Season

Know this, my heart, let love go hunting free,
Nor ever seek to stay him from the game,
And guard the lips from any rash decree —
(A woman never sees such things the same.)
Let love go free, but leave the latch-string out,
And keep the supper hot, the fireplace bright;
And sing a cheerful song to banish doubt,
To spread a welcome through the gathering night.

So ask no questions, voice no shrill alarm,
For love will always seek a happy place;
Your anguish cannot ward away all harm,
And kisses ill befall a tear-stained face.
Then quick, away, these tears; arrange this hair;
Throw wide the door, his foot is on the stair.

Ethel Case Cook
Eagle River, Wisconsin

Counterpoint

Rain came at dawn
along with the ringing
of the telephone.
Her symphony had stilled
while silver showers sang
against the window.
The children were rowdy
and rampant with life.
Outside, a mourning dove
crooned counterpoint
around their normalcy.

J. Karyl Arnold
Medina, Ohio

Bittersweet

Oh, Bittersweet, the pain that comes,
   When two hearts,
   Once one,
   Beat again,
   Each upon its own.
   When two lives,
   For a time interwoven,
   Become single threads,
   That will not mesh again.
   When two people,
   Once lovers,
   Become friends.

Barbara Kee Vatovec
Marion, Illinois

Solo Flight

now that I'm preparing
to blast off out of your orbit
into my own world
you're turning on the charm
and diluting my fuel
of hurt and anger

but you forfeited your right
to interfere with my flight plan
when you moved in with another
and my departure date is set

this is a solo flight

Jennifer Becker
Independence, Missouri

When Gone the Flame

The tacky air
clung thick between us.
With clamped arms folded,
our puffed-up faces
pooched preposterous pouts
at one another,
and a silent coating
vaguely draped
our stiffened stances
like hardening candlewax
dripping down
a burned out candle.

Nancy Brier O'Neal
Cuero, Texas

Insomnus

Clover candles by my window
    Cast soft shadows into
My dreams. . .
    Tonight, their sad, sweet smell
Wafts down around my pillow
    Caressing my face and hair
'til I can bear the distance
    no longer and am drawn
like a moth to beat my wings
    at their serenity.
Such softnesses flood into my mind
    and overflow —
A pool of wax spilling onto the floor.

Krista Werner
Springfield, Illinois

Like a Single Leaf

My heart weeps like the winter rain;
    it sighs with the wind.
As a sagging door on rusty hinges,
    it moans.

The naked lines of naked branches
    rake the bitter blue
clawing the emptiness.

My heart is as forlorn as the empty nest,
    swinging sadly,
waiting for Spring's new arrivals.

As desperate as the single leaf
    still clinging to its slender branch.

Janet Rahmani
Red Oak, Iowa

Unruly Intruder

Why come back now
when I have re-arranged
the turbulence and tumult
to a calm my soul can live with?
You, unencumbered, I would welcome in
and set the kettle on for brewing tea,
remove your dust-stained coat
and fold my hands
to listen to the mazed, unwinding tale
of your long absences.
You, unencumbered, yes — but not the pack
of wild, unruly memories that leap and snarl,
upset the careful arrangement
of my most private rooms,
and then close in with snapping jaws
to howl triumphant victory
above the shreds and tatters that were me.

Alice Mackenzie Swaim
Harrisburg, Pennsylvania

Within Depression's Grasp

Interred was she
Amid the only furniture they'd ever bought —
Red naugahyde accent chair,
Brown naugahyde sofa,
Solid birch dining table with four fine chairs
With green naugahyde seats.
Such things last forever
And never wear out.
Just people wear out.
She walks around his stolid silence
Around the vault of his inner self
And feels the cold bricks of his exterior
And hears the clang of closing doors.

Betty Jane Sachara
Gilroy, California

Disintegration

Particles of my being
Unattached
Falling away
Leaving less now
Where nothing was before

Karla J. Ziesemer
Beatrice, Nebraska

Chapter 6

Anniversary

Late summer . . .
goldenrod, Queen Anne's Lace
and slow sound of crickets
acorns dropping, locusts drowsing

Now . . .
between the early harvest and late
we were married . . .
Clouds slanted over the lake
and rain came, as if to tell us
time is long, and forgiving

Since then . . .
each year, at this time
we have gone off into the hills
on some small adventure
together . . . alone . . .
and renewed our vows . . .

Our last August
was spent in your hospital room
They brought us a cake marked with "65"
and made merry
but I held your hand under the covers
and looked, through haze
to the mountains

Kathleen W. Ela
Rochester, Wisconsin

Vigil

I pad silently to your side.
"I'm cold," you breathe past the demerol.
I tuck the granny afghan around you
(Remember how we always called it magic?
We've run out of magic tricks, haven't we?).
Your hands and arms are already cooling,
swelling, just as the doctor warned they would,
and I know it won't be long.
I purr courage in your drugged ear,
half to comfort you, half to comfort me.
Oh, God, if I could only snatch you back
from malignant doors that opened one by one,
closed you inside, shut me outside caterwauling,
shivering out our last brief night.
Your smile blossoms through synthetic slumber
as I rub up against you lovingly . . . .
waiting . . . . waiting . . . . it won't be long:
death lies across your feet like a cat.

Christine Christian
Forest City, Iowa

FIFTH PLACE POEM

Prayer Over An Old Photograph

Suddenly! I see you
fresh, so little
and new; the
impact of promise
breathtaking & scary.
I wanted it
to be easier
for you babe
not harder. Watching your mind
riddled from pain
my mind grabs at air
frantic as beached trout, words
jumbling into anger & sorrow
helpless as grace.

You are grieving/I am grieving.

I want you
to know this: please
carry it with you
to take out
to look at
when your pulse
touches thunder
and you hear
silence shrieking curses
only your heart hears; know
that life minus darkness
is what I have wished you,
garlands swirling around you,
a strawberry season.

Yes! always birds singing/do you
hear birds singing?

Sherrill Morgan Finn
New Hartford, Connecticut

Pax Tecum
Et Lux Eterna

for Raymond Roseliep, Priest and Poet
  (1917-1983)

Master of Haiku,
I pen for you this farewell
as the cold year dies.

Rabbit in the Moon
was your joyous final book.
I read and cherish

your words as I read
and cherish your gallant life
your soaring spirit

and your potent verse;
all the human condition
was part of your art,

yet hope never died;
surely God's eternal light
is your bright reward

Will C. Jumper
Ames, Iowa

Alone

The pale, cold, tired face,
Her listless arms in an empty embrace.
Colorless hair, at last flowing free,
Eyes veiled by darkness, longing to see.
Lying in silence; in peace, forsooth,
Her every dream shattered, all bits of truth.
Surrounded by the hues of blooming wildflowers,
She waits in the field for long, lonely hours
When she rises from her grave, she gazes down below,
And the rainbow over her head is her shining halo.

Beth Welden
Iowa Falls, Iowa
Age 15

Stars

I am like a star,
lonely and shy,
trying to find myself.
For I do not shine my light through the
    universe.
I want to stand
strong and bold,
and be an individual,
but I'm lost.
All I can do is show my inner light.
I am eternally searching.

Jennifer Ryan
Honor, Michigan
Age 10, Grade 4

October Rose

When the frost is
On the pumpkin
It is also on the rose —
A rose, not as fragile
As we usually suppose
Sturdy, strong yet delicate
October's beauty just begun —
Pink, snow-edged, defiant
Lovely in an Indian summer sun
Swaying in the autumnal breeze
Morning frost to dew transformed
Escaping a deeper freeze
When the frost is
On the pumpkin,
And also on the rose.

Sister Monica Lammers
Detroit Lakes, Minnesota

Of Robes for Rituals

In the armoires of memory and dream,
they hang in careful rows
for savoring, pomander-scented,
the garments of my days, past or unworn.
At hours when time stands still
and wild storms beat
against my shuttered windows,
I dress up
in varied colors of remembered joy.
I try on robes of strange arcane design,
patterned for rituals;
test them for fit, plan which to wear
for ceremonies of ungauged tomorrows.

Alice Mackenzie Swaim
Harrisburg, Pennsylvania

The Sun

Its rays of light
Pierce the Earth.
It reaches us within
And tranquilizes sorrow.
And then it gallops
To hide behind the moon.

Andrew Corson
Iowa Falls, Iowa
Age 15

Ghost Moon

Ghost moon sits hazy
In the day sky,
Being a mere shadow
Of its totality,
Seeming half an entity,
Split, dissected, un-whole
As if in wait for the heavens
To spin and weave
Its other face.

This spirit rises to join
Its orbital plight of incompleteness,
Feeling an obscure camaraderie
With the lingering half,
Sensing with it a severance
An aloneness, yet not realizing
'Tis only an illusion.

For that lunar sphere
Is truly round and full,
Having substance on all sides
And depth within
Just as does this heart
Of mine.

Beth Helen Nowell
Carmel, California

Salute to America
Upon the Fourth of July:
An Immigrant Remembers

Bleak ocean crossing
Cargo of memory
Of warm tropic nights
My mother's pale
Perspiring grief
My old dog's dumb
Confusion.

Three jobs tired
Eighteen months afraid
Within my mailbox
I'd glimpse
Official ink —
Illegal.

Yet in America
It was
I put some flesh
Upon the spirit
Of my dreams.

Patricia J. Hoad
Princeton, New Jersey

Hope

The mountain
Draws near,
Ebbs again to nothing.
Do I seek stability
From sea and air?
Do I expect
The earth to soar?

J. M. Frank
Seattle, Washington

Dawn Flight

Up through the dark indigo spread
Of furrowing, orange flecked stratus,
Wings, struts, and fuselage glazing —
I climb within the great pale dome,
High in the thinning air, flying
In lemon light toward fading stars:
Alone, racing the mountain dawn,
And time, quickening in rebirth.

Arthur C. Frick
Waverly, Iowa

Glacier

The ice is brighter than the sun, a slab
Miles deep, its edge a jagged smile
On the mountain's face. But something breaks
It. Remember the sound of the calving. ("Calving", as though
A birth.) Huge white shards crack
Like thunder, and sink glittering into the sea.

The ocean sinks beneath us, rises, sinks,
Rises, and we walk trembling on the gasping
Sea as the light splits and splits and splits again.

Jim Albright
Bryan, Ohio

Risk

Unexpectedly,
The adventures we would seek
Lie in wait
At some prosaic crossroad,
Uniquely unsought —
Unsupposed.

Arthur C. Frick
Waverly, Iowa

Frostfire

Brittle reeds of sedge,
Steps breaking crisp
Crowns of white fire.
Branches empty, bony
Fingers scratching the
Gray slate-hard sky.
Bird nests fallen hollow,
Brown feathers trembling,
Tipped with snow.
Faces, misty, dreaming,
Lost in cold, swirling fog —
Or etched fine, sharp
Diamond-bright in frost.
Bird wings flapping black
Shadows in the white, mirrory morning.
Crawing emptily in the cold,
Windy caverns of the mind.
Streets — hushed, empty, lone.
People driven like tumbleweed,
Bundled warm in clothes
And dark winter secrets.
Beggars' gnarled, blue hands
Outstretched emptily over flat miles,
Clutching quick as if to hold
The fleeing ice-blue gleams
Of still, white winter stars.

Frank Tropea
Brighton, Massachussetts

An Image of Spring

I walk
through a dreamlike mist
of crabapples' cascading petals,
pink and white,
whirling and dancing
in the early springtime breeze,
And my thoughts turn to you —
how like the flowering trees
we too are blossoming.

Tracy Grandy
Cedar Falls, Iowa

Signs of Spring

A gentle breeze blowing against your face
Small buds blooming on a locust tree
Wet green grass shining beneath your feet
Slimy black mud along the riverside
Robins sweetly singing in the high tree-tops
Soft green-yellow moss clinging toughly to the rock-walls
April showers sprinkling into ponds, and lakes,
               filling them slowly
Gleaming carp, and perch shining under the sun's light
Cool, lonely nights below the full moon
Small pussy-willows feel soft against your face
Tiny flowers blooming in the sun's warmth.

Douglas Pfeiffer
Danbury, Connecticut
Age 10

Butterfly

Nature's
    young,
     velvet
butterfly
    floating,
     gliding,
evoking beauty

and yet, not even trying to.

Wayne C. Burgess
Sheldon, Illinois

God's Living Jewel

Feathered prism,
Living rainbow,
Reflected sunlight,
   Jewel on wings.
Refracted light like cut diamonds.
Darting, dashing —
   Nature's over-achiever.
Aerialist,
Stunt pilot,
Gyrator,
Helicopter,
Living Jewel —
   The Hummingbird

Alex A. Widicker
St. Helena, California

Rose Lawn Cemetery

Dog-bark echoes,
locust screams,
tiny bird heads
kissing gravel
in a light rain —
a night simmers
while the dead snore
in no certain
state of somnolence.

    Clouds like smoke
    move across the sky,
    carrying a darkness
    that is contained in your eyes,
    a darkness I may never understand.

Laced with green,
stone blocks stand
in summer heat
while lightning bugs
wander,
lighting onto
limestone crosses and
the lichen-filled crevices
of praying hands.

    In search of my holiness
    I entered that darkness
    for a moment.
    In search of my holiness
    I fell into the pit of your eyes
    and writhed like a
    bug on its back.

It is a night heavy
with moisture and the
breath of worms,
the clawing of the air
by six tiny legs,

the final flutter of moth wings
against a lampshade.

>You knew only one song,
>played only one melody
>so secretly and silently
>to yourself.
>Your instrument finely tuned,
>you greeted the warm night
>with your notes,
>intricately placed in trees,
>under rocks,
>out of view, out of reach.

It is a night reeking of
the underside of things,
for I have enfolded myself in
some dark wing
and will careen through
this night sky,
laced with gin and stars.

Margaret Brady
Chicago Heights, Illinois

Flash

I am a terrific, fantastic star.
I'm blue, red, yellow, and white.
I make images in the sky,
of lions, dippers, and people.
I'm filled with inner-light that makes me
feel warm and wonderful.

Jason Hobson
Interlochen, Michigan
Age 8, Grade 2

Transition

Children sing silver sounds
of soft brilliance. Sheer translucent
notes float lightly like soap bubbles
blown at a party
with laughter
which soon fades into silence.
Like notes.

Leslie H. Fishel, Jr.
Fremont, Ohio

Waterfall Variations

Jump
Up and
Land
In an
Elfland salty water of
               a sea miden's lair
                which will haunt you
                  on and on
                    until you deal with
Bravery making your heart beat
With the sound
Of a waterfall

Sorrow
Entering into
An unusual,
Tinted, waterfall pool makes
Beauty something that feels
Like untouchable laughter

Julie Stratton
City, Michigan

Bedtime

When I go to sleep at night
my blankets are like soft kittens
that make me warm.
I feel calm, safe, and secure.
When I close my eyes
I see fairies with red tulip dresses,
little buttercups for crowns,
and little sticks for wands
that twinkle with magic when the fairies
wave them.
I feel like I am floating on a gentle sea
when I drift off to sleep.

Sara Sheppard Szymanski
Beulah, Michigan
Age 7

Contentment

A rainbow's misty colors decorate
the sky with shifting patterns.
Birds sing . . . a warm sunbeam
caresses my face . . . the grass is
fragrant and alive with insects,
decorated; beautified by flowers.
A nearby stream bubbles, giggles,
and churns.
I rejoice . . . I am alive . . .
I am content.

Sarah Jaquish
Interlochen, Michigan
Age 11

The Dancer

Black ballet slippers rest unoccupied
on the worn dance floor
as the odor of week-old perspiration
lingers in the room.

A dark skinned woman stands,
motionless, near the broken window —
her muscles taut even though
she rests.

She peers down
on the wet, musty street below
only to see
the darkness of the night.

Wiping water droplets from her cheek,
she slowly stretches
her perfect body
to its never existing limit.

Lisa M. Billman
Tolono, Illinois

Poem For The New York City Ballet

Balancing my thoughts
on top of my head
Pointing my toes
I lift my arms
like the wings
of a potted pigeon
circling Central Park.

Claudia Hochberg
Dallas, Texas

Child at the Symphony

They sat me down
amid *allegro non troppo* and *con brio*
the sound settling softly
into my being. Evening after evening
themes and variations at the symphony.
They expected me to squirm, one
too young to read the program,
but there were things for the eye:
> the rise and fall of bows in rows,
> a swaying of the glitter-horns,
> pale men at drums, half hidden.

One concert well remembered:
as the conductor flipped his pages
I counted them, aloud,
winning nearby smiles but
dark frowns from parents.

There were disciplines in the air
like phantom teachers. Instructions
imprinted on interiors.

Musicians to this day
find me fit to listen
with knowing ear, trained only
as a drafted and unknowing child

Darrell H. Bartee
Wichita, Kansas

Sea Wife, Waiting

Now your kayak fades
over the rim of the world
to some forever-place.
You will know the wind,
the unforgiving sea,
and I shall walk alone
where the sea-gull mourns.

Westering, the sun
dies in living flame.
and on the signal cliff
I must set the fire;
eastward, darkness lies . . . .
the birds are silent now,
and in all this lonely land
your singing voice is lost.

Jessie Eastman Holt
Prairie du Chien, Wisconsin

Bearance

Was it a fragment of a moment gone
Or was it beginning of eternity,
When, through salty, clammy mist, I
Watched the majestic ship move slowly,
Gracefully out to sea? A tall man in
Sailor's garb suddenly was there where
He said he'd be, leaning on the enclosing
Rail. His eyes and wave electrified the
Air above the ever widening, sweeping
Waves. Then he turned and disappeared
Behind a mass of blurred and formless,
Meaningless humanity frozen in a state
Of nauseous drab. Vocal cords congealed.
He would not hear. Zero count-down was
Here before another dawn.
So much was left undone!

A bone-penetrating vapor gray consumed
The embryo of hope. A journey's longed-for
Inception and question-filled termination
Floated quietly, swiftly far away from me.
Would a tomorrow come?

Dorothy Moore
Dowagiac, Michigan

The Paper Court

If I could find the secret of that chained youth
Bitter adolescence, simmering in mediocrity only
Half understood and tracing the flaked paint
On the front door with wonder, not knowing we
Were poor, I might have courage now to pull
That portal wide. Once inside, I'd climb again
The hall coat rack with dark and curious hooks
Look once and then away from that dim mirror
Oval of black magic for reflecting other days.

Times of casual invincibility, enjoying *droit*
Du seigneur in mythic kingdom only I could know,
Trading my right for that insistent loneliness
Made worse because I thought that I alone was
Lonely. Still catching blindly at a few
Unclouded joys of safe and secret satisfactions.
Another generation would explain my Oedipal
Delights — I only knew them. Yet they seemed
Small enough when balanced with the price I paid
In painful questions with no answer. These
Troubled times I need not know again.

As I count years and confidently now
Accept the differences between myself and any
Other — all in my mind, I say — the fabric of
The universe is changed. When young the company
Of all vague others in the world (put there,
I thought, to make me feel more real) could only
Emphasize the differences. But from my distance
Then *they* captured all the prizes, were the best,
The enchanted, doing no work, but floating
Free above the populace, not seeing me.

"Best writer," "Most beautiful," "Best dancer,"
I did not aspire to one of these — I took them
All into that private dream. I'd be them all.
There, I was infrangible, perfect in surface and
Resource. Years must have darkened more
That hat-rack mirror — but strangely mummified the

Image of the perfect princess lives, her paper
Court a two-dimensional kingdom marching past.
The cadence of faint music heard is custom
Composition for this last last visit home.

E. Matthew Lewis
Ft. Lauderdale, Florida

HONORABLE MENTION

Becoming

Classic Redwood
   ever green and stalwart
     weathered by ages
   yet gracious in undeniable poise
Maturity borne of patience
   through Nature's thoughtlessness
Never boasting . . .
   quietly being.
     Such unaffected reign!
Rich with bearing
   and well-learned season,
Sequoia revels in its becoming;
   Inspiration to saplings
     with sights upturned in awe
Smiling its peace
   to tired oaks
     that sigh in respect.

Bonnie L. Thomas
San Jose, California

From Out of the Blue

From out of beyond came music to me,
a haunting sound from another sphere.
The music lifted me out of myself
whipsering faintly, 'tis only a step,
from out of the here and into there.
I listened closely, I wanted to hear
that haunting music ringing clear.
But it only lasted a moment more
then I was back on my earthly shore.
Now I gladly wait for that haunting call
Where life is no mystery after all
then off I'll fly with never a tear
to that musical, haunting soul-fed sphere.

Vernelia B. Jobe
Endeavor, Wisconsin

Dawn Flight

Up through the dark indigo spread
Of furrowing, orange flecked stratus,
Wings, struts, and fuselage glazing —
I climb within the great pale dome,
High in the thinning air, flying
In lemon light toward fading stars:
Alone, racing the mountain dawn,
And time, quickening in rebirth.

Arthur C. Frick
Waverly, Iowa

Night Surf

White crests rise from a black expanse of sea,
Spurred on by winds far distant from the land.
They peak and peak again, then shoreward roll
To dissipate at last upon the sand.

The ageless, anguished voices of the deep
Are echoed in the roiling water's roar;
And vaguely, through the darkness, we can hear
Old chanties sung by mariners of yore.

Then dawn must come. The rising sun shines gold
Upon the breaking waves that never cease.
But somehow day surf just cannot compare
With night surf and its countless mysteries.

Kathryn Gelander
Oregon, Illinois

Aging

Walking is too staid
To contain the ecstasy one feels in being alive.
Rather one must run like a child
In sheer exuberance.

It's been long since I ran from pure excess of joy
Or raced for the mere delight in motion.

For now my snail body must strive to keep pace,
To bound with my antelope spirit.

Meg Kramer
Truman, Minnesota

Within My Shut Eyes

I see first red,
then colors graying to black.
Inside myself a spot shines
and opens, blossoming.
This seed of light
joins me with others
as separate plants
are rooted into soil
by some shared power.
The bright flow like water
reaches me in shiny fingers, nourishing.
My dryness is quenched,
my wonder fed.

Jean Kennedy
Waterloo, Iowa

Patterns in the Sand

Your inner-self drifts
like waves making patterns in the sand.
Your soul dances in the sky
like a tiny ballerina.
Your dreams fly and are
lost in the wind.
Your mind departs
like a bird soaring over an open field
never to return again.

Christy Revnell
Honor, Michigan
Age 10

Gone Was My Night

Early,
Before the world arose,
Skies were black
And I felt a thousand burdens;
Then I walked a flowered meadow
Where faith erased doubt,
And gone was my night!

Maude G. Booth
Marble, Minnesota

Springfire

Like fires of Spring
burning dead grass
from seasons past,
set me aflame,
Holy Spirit.

Purge me from wastes
of yesterday
but keep alive,
in my heart,
embers of truth

to glow again,
radiating Your warmth
toward the stranger
searching
for peace.

Dolly Redden
Rossville, Illinois

Chapter 7

The Fire Next Time

I am old
Seventeen billion years old
Having begun with primoridal fire
And afraid for fire again

Old matter
Having burst into being
Hydrogen born and helium
Gathered into starlight

Creating space
And light in the darkness
Gathering the fundament round
Earth places other places

And I live now
Green and growing
And I think about myself
As I could not then

Stars give birth
To sunlight and children
Playing on the grass
My children

Here and there
Where life is born
And matter thinks long thoughts
About itself

Long thoughts
Probing the hidden ways
For nuclear secrets
And fire

I am old
Having come to life
Glad for perspective and afraid
For the first time.

Conrad Simonson
Decorah, Iowa

ships waiting at vung tao — circa 1966

oh hear this saigon soldier vietnam
i have seen your sampans sailing among the war
ships at vung tao
i have eaten your rice and nuc man from little
porcelain bowls
celebrated love with you upon straw mat beds
kissed the golden faces of your children
inhaled the transcending essences of your opium
listened to the rigadoon of life
in your hearts
and in your streets
and have climbed the hills
above your villages
to stand before
your venerated effigy
of buddha
to look into your soul
and shout
to all who would hear
you and i
are one
we are one

dennis torres
malibu, california

The Locked Ward (August 3, 1980)

With the poison out of my veins,
the tears drowned in a deeper misery,
the door shuts like any other door,
but the lock clicks as the bolt drives home,
the sound as final as the act was meant to be
that culminates in this quiet place of light colors,
nurses in patchwork smocks and telltale white shoes,
others whose blank eyes do not reflect my panic,
my dread, my relief that something has finally ended.
Among the Stelazine zombies, I wait like the Phoenix,
stirring the tepid ashes with my pointed toe.
The fire has cleansed me.
I am light, empty of ambition and desire.
Only regret holds me down.
It will tarnish my wings when I rise again, scarred but new.
The fire never purges that it does not leave its mark,
the brand that says: I was damned but have found the lost
    way back.

But for now I sit in dull anguish.
I am outside myself, waiting,
dispassionate while my heart thuds and misses,
fighting for the pattern that has been disrupted.
A slender boy with fine, red hair, blue eyes drugged and
    blank,
stares at me unseeing, and I wonder:
Where did I first step so surely on the road that brought me
    here?

Did I break down, shatter like a dropped mirror,
or finally just bend my neck to the inevitable,
kneel before it, resigned,
parting my hair for the terrible steel of necessity,
throwing my arms wide in supplication?
I give myself up to this place,
I trade my years-long struggle for a measure of peace,

a few days to let myself float on the bottom,
staring up at the surface that shimmers and refracts,
that is as distant and fragmented as the world outside the door.
Consumed by fire, drowned, cloven cleanly by my own headsman's ax,
I wait.
Among the shuffling feet, the nurses' veiled eyes,
the drugged, bruised vacancy of red-lashed, sky-blue eyes,
I see my own shadow move with infinite weariness and relief
to take its place.

Ann Caroline Kabel
Obernburg am Main, West Germany

THIRD PLACE POEM

Snow

Its white tranquility
Surfaces our emotions,
Conveying our thoughts
Through the oblivion of time and space.
Its soft innocence
Is but a disguise for its power —
The power that crumbles the wall
And sends us to freedom.

Andrew Corson
Iowa Falls, Iowa
Age 15

Requiescat

Death appears in patches
at the foot of the bed.
Scraps of shape here and there;
patterns of almost seen design.
At given intervals little splats
separate and move down to
lie disguised as a wrinkle
on the blanket or a small stain.
Inching forward the front end makes
room for the back and the whole
lies pleated on the sheets,
sucking itself in and
growing longer, its colors merge
as it drapes itself around the
walls of skin, creeping over
legs and groin and in it goes
and up through sex and bowels,
rotating itself, in no hurry
for it doesn't want to rush now
but inexorably onward until
with a single throe it and you
and all those colors blend
into one pattern
and are gone.

Caroline St. Julien
Milwaukee, Wisconsin

Motifs

The archaic symbols of the dream
appear nightly stained on some
gigantic scrim.
There's a battle going on in one corner,
a damsel is at stake; her favors
his reward of course.
Somewhere else is a monkey
holding a tin cup and
pant-hooting at passers-by.
There will be some trouble if he
doesn't get his pennies.
More, I suppose, if he does.

A man and a woman face each other;
she prepares bandages for his war.
The problem is she can't
reach the victims he
piles up.

Birds fly, horses fly, lizards slither
out of holes each with pieces of paper
fluttering from their mouths. The paper
disappears leaving only sockets
without sound.

The dream is incomplete without the man
in the middle, standing still.
He cannot move and the tears

on his face are children.

Caroline St. Julien
Milwaukee, Wisconsin

SECOND PLACE POEM

Cain's Children

For millenia seeded
father to son,
some genetic memory
troubles the mind of man,
    takes him unaware
on the edge of a thought,
and suddenly lonely,
alien to Earth,
for one blazing moment
he recalls
the far horizon
    of a loved, forbidden land.
Then achingly, he knows
his own true continent.

    But now the way is lost,
on Earth no sign remains,
so he probes the sky,
computes the galaxies,
hoping to find
beyond some flaring star
the half-remembered road
of his desire.

Jessie Eastman Holt
Prairie du Chien, Wisconsin

The Postlude

     I shall not talk with other guards tonight
About weaponry and technique,
Nor with elevator operators
Of grievances or fishing.
Nor shall I wander the basement maze
with my pocket radio, seeking reception.
     Instead I shall finish the night alone
In the chill air of the bank loading dock
Looking out over the beginnings
Of its future parking ramp.
Two blocks away a crane swings its
Wrecking ball against another building.
I hear the diesel, and the hum,
The moans, the sighs, and the soft, thick squeals,
The subtle changes of pitch, and organ tones,
A thud, and a little spill of bricks.
All this in a fine sequence
That repeats over and over
Through the night, night after night.
It is not violent, but keening.
It is the sweetest, saddest music that I know.
It sings to my bones. I shall listen until dawn.

       — *security guard, St. Paul, 1978*

Jeff Wright
Prairie du Chien, Wisconsin

HONORABLE MENTION

Judges

Charlotte H. Bruner is a professor of French and coordinator of "Third-World Cultures" at Iowa State University. She has published critical articles and translations of francophone poets of Africa and the Caribbean. She selected and edited *Unwinding Trends: Writing by Women in Africa* (Heinemann, New Hampshire and London, 1983, 1984). She and her husband, David, produce a series of programs called "Third Person Feminine" on WOI-Radio.

David K. Bruner, Professor Emerictus, English, Iowa State University in Ames, was born in 1912 in St. Louis, Missouri. He received B.A. And M.A. degrees from Washington University and a Ph.D from the University of Illinois. "First Person Feminine," the radio program he does with his wife, Charlotte, consists of interviews, readings, and commentary on contemporary Third World writers.

Marsha Conn has a master of arts degree in museum and art education. She teaches English in the Chicago school system and travels widely around the world.

Will C. Jumper, a professor of English at Iowa Statue University in Ames, did his undergraduate study in chemistry at the University of California in Berkeley. While teaching high school at Modesto, California, he earned his M.A. in creative writing and his Ph.D in American literature at Stanford. He has published short stories, poems, and critical essays widely and has one book of poetry, *From Time Remembered,* 1977.

Jean Kennedy teaches writing courses at the University of Northern Iowa, Cedar Falls, writes poetry and fiction, edits for a U.N.I. colleague, keeps the family calendar straight (three children). She received her M.A. from Northwestern University and considers herself an all-purpose writer because of her work on newspapers and technical journals. She has taught creative writing to Senior Citizens for the Iowa Arts Council and to the children with the Gifted and Talented Program of the Waterloo Schools.

Daniel M. McGuiness lives in Iowa Falls, where he teaches English at Ellsworth College. He also directs the Ellsworth Poetry Project, a series of readings and workshops on the campus. Currently he is nearing completion of his Ph.D dissertation on modern poetry at the University of Iowa.

Sarah P. Simmons lives part-time in Cedar Rapids, Iowa, where she periodically attends the University of Iowa, and part-time in Washington, D.C., where she rides horses in nearby country and weaves in and out of city traffic on a bicycle. She is a volunteer librarian at St. Elizabeths Hospital and worked as a volunteer in one of the capital city's soup kitchens. Her life strongly influenced by the writings of William Stafford and Nikos Kazantzakis, she has studied with Stafford. Published in all prior CSS Publications poetry anthologies, this is her third time acting as a judge for the contests. She expects to have her first book of poems, *A Hook in Its Mouth,* published this year by CSS Publications.

Curt L. Sytsma is an attorney at law, a syndicated newspaper poet, author of *The Rhyme & Reason of Curt Sytsma,* instructor of advanced legal writing at Drake University, and the father of Justin, featured elsewhere in this anthology.

Contributors

Tammy Rayne Abbey, 22, divides her time between work, karate, community theatre, and reading anything and everything.

Tina Abolins, a graduate from Grand View College with a B.A. in graphic design, is anxious and ambitious to pursue a challenging career. "Poetry is a special way of expressing with words. It leaves an impression, like a painting."

Jim Albright, 35, is a minister and a father of three. He is an outdoorsman and a singer and storyteller as well as a poet.

Ronald L. "Andy" Andrzejewski is currently teaching Dale Carnegie Courses in Western Michigan. Published a dozen times coast to coast, this is his third appearance with CSS Publications. He feels that "being published is the greatest method of gaining immortality ever devised."

Corinne B. Ansell has come through a great Depression, a World War, taught schoolchildren, raised a family, and is enjoying her granchildren. She knows forests, lakes, snow, rain, and sunshine; she looks forward to writing.

Ivan Arguelles, of Mexican-American heritage, is the author of several poetry collections, the latest *Manicomio*. Employed as a librarian at the University of California, he resides in Berkeley.

J. Karyl Arnold is a professional poet, fiction writer, and literary agent. She and her husband operate "The Wordsmith" from their home. Karyl is co-publicity director of Ohio Poetry Day Association. This is her third year in a CSS Publications anthology.

Marie A. Asner, 42, is a private music instructor in Shawnee, Kansas. Recently, she received a doctorate in music education and is currently celebrating her 30th year as a church organist.

Darrell H. Bartee, 77, has worked as a writer in Colorado, Kansas, and New York. A former small-town newspaper editor and Peace Corps volunteer, he declines to retire.

Jennifer Becker, a freelance editor and typographer, likes to travel and hopes a trip to Europe will be possible in the near future.

Noni Bookbinder Bell, 25, was raised in New York City but now lives in the Pine Barrens of New Jersey where she, her husband and a partner have a commercial waterproofing corporation; they restore high rises in New York City. But, "through all that I am still a poet."

Enid M. Bennett, 84, is a retired teacher, mother, grandmother and great-grandmother who has lived on a small farm in the same house for 61 years. She has traveled in each of the 50 states, in Mexico and in Canada. She likes to do woodcarving, sculpture, and oil painting. This is her seventh appearance in a CSS Publications anthology.

Jack Bernier belongs to seven state poetry societies. His poetry has been published by American Poetry Association, San Fernando Poetry Journal, Hoosier Challenger, Poetry Press, Dan River Press, Tarragon Publications, and Potpourri International. He has won many second to fifth place awards.

Lisa M. Billman, 22, is a physical education teacher and coach in Woodstock, Illinois. She has been writing poetry for seven years; three other poems have been published.

Karen Black, a graduate of Iowa State University, is the mother of two teenagers, an elementary teacher, and a part-time clown. She has begun a business of writing and illustrating clown greeting cards with her character, Hildy, as the theme.

Maude G. Booth, 74, is a mother, grandmother, and great-grandmother who began writing poetry 20 years ago. A member of Arrowhead Poetry Society and Minnesota League of Poets, she writes on varied subjects in many forms.

Catherine Boulanger, the mother of five boys, holds a B.A. from Luther College and an M.A. from Southern Illinois University at Carbondale; for the past six years, she has been a Spanish teacher at St. Paul High School. She has been writing poetry for about 20 years.

Margaret Brady, 28, is a freelance journalist currently employed in the public relations field. She has been writing poetry for 10 years.

Laurre Breman, 30, is a self-employed social worker who writes poetry and stories in her spare time. An extensive traveler, she has just returned from Scandinavia. "I hope to place a touch of 'the mountain king' in my works yet to come."

Doris T. Brokaw finds that researching and tracking along the path to a poem is high adventure. This is her fifth appearance in a CSS Publications anthology.

Dale Bryant, 41, is a freelance writer and has just enrolled in the graduate English program at San Jose State University. This is her second appearance in a CSS Publications anthology.

Wayne C. Brugess, 33, has been writing poetry since grade school. Recently, he has combined his photographic talents with his poetry and has begun illustrating his poems for publication.

Joan Merryman Burns lives with her husband on an acreage in central Georgia. Fifteen Shetland ponies and numerous kinds of poultry share the land, still terraced from the days of cotton and black labor.

Sharon L. Buettell is a wife, a mother of five (four of them teenagers), and a full-time secretary. Writing poetry, started as a lark five years ago, is developing into a hobby of serious intent.

Sheryl Carlon, 31, is an artist and mother of two children. Her home is in the woods of northern Minnesota.

Myrtle T. Cavallo authored the Danbury Poetry Chapter motto: "Poetry unread/Is dead." She has a teacher son, is an avid reader, loves the theatre, art, music and, naturally, poetry.

R. J. Caylor, 47, enjoys reading, music, swimming, people, and writing poetry. He has had several poems published (this is his third appearance in a CSS Publications anthology) and does his best composition while driving at night.

Virgil Chahre, 35, is a graduate of the University of Wyoming. He has more than 30 poems published and two books of poetry in print.

Lynne A. Chapman lives on Port Bay in Wolcott, New York, with her three-year-old daughter Crickey. She has been writing poetry for seven years, this is her second published poem.

Christine Christian believes creative people are like dandelions: "steadied by long tap root, we add texture and color to an otherwise bluegrass existence. We must continue blowing our seeds on the bare spots of life."

Ethel Case Cook, 73, has been a poet since grade school and an R.N. since 1931. She's still active in both fields and in volunteerism. Her first love is people. She was selected in 1982 as one of the 10 most admired senior citizens in Wisconsin.

Andrew Corson enjoys long-distance bicycling, cross-country skiing, juggling, unicycling, and writing poetry and prose for fun. His future plans include the study of literature and composition in college and a possible teaching career.

Jennifer Riddle Cupples, 6, lives on a farm near Lac Me'gantic, Quebec. Among other interests, she enjoys being a member of the Ranger Rick Club and playing with her baby brother. This is her first poem.

Linda Curtis, 48, of Urbandale, Iowa, aspires "to be that poet who follows the press around while they follow the politicians. You know. What's-her-name?" This is her seventh appearance in a CSS Publications anthology.

Linda Lee Curtis of Phoenix, Arizona, has written six books of poetry. Also, she writes songs and recently published a "self-help" book, *Money-Making Ideas for Poets.*

Andrew W. Dawson, 38, wrote "Threnody" two weeks after his father (a close friend) died. This is his first published poem and his goal is to write fiction.

Jeff T. Dick, 29, is a native Iowan who returned from two years in Los Angeles to attend the University of Iowa as a graduate student in library and information science.

Margery Disburg, widow and church secretary, has been writing for 25 years. Mother of three, grandmother of four, she enjoys reading, theatre, and talking with other poets.

Jennifer Dongvillo, 11, is a sixth grade student at Platte River Elementary School. She is an avid reader and enjoys singing, dancing, piano, sewing, art, and writing.

Esther Edleman, retired school teacher, finds fulfillment and joy in composing and sharing her verses. "It has been exciting to watch the rapid growth of CSS Publications and to be a small part of it." She has been published in all seven CSS Publications anthologies.

Joan Edwards, 51, starts life anew with two artificial hips successfully implanted in December, 1983. She and her husband have moved into a smaller home with two of their four children.

Mike Eldon, 39, runs a computer company in Kenya, where he lives with his Iowa-born wife and two children. Having helped *Cut from the Wave,* he is thrilled to be in *Need.*

Jerri Evans started writing poetry in high school for the school newspaper. After a local writer's group was formed, she started writing and submitting poetry again; she has published in Iowa, Washington, D.C., and California.

Kathleen W. Ela, 42, writes, gardens, edits a local poetry column, collects phenological data, studies haiku, and sometimes helps her orchardist husband pick apples. She has five children. This is her fifth consecutive appearance in a CSS Publications anthology.

Charles Fabrizio has had poems published in several little magazines and anthologies. While continuing to pursue his poetic and screenplay efforts, he is saving up to buy the Empire State Building.

Michael Felsburg, 11, is in the sixth grade at Platte River School. He lives in Honor, Michigan.

Sherill Morgan Finn writes poetry to stay balanced. She has had 11 poems published and won three honorable mentions. She will be producing a poetry series for cablevision in the fall of 1984.

Brian Finney's poetry has been published in a variety of anthologies and literary magazines through the Midwest and California. This is his third appearance in a CSS Publications anthology.

Leslie H. Fishel, Jr., was educated at Oberlin and Harvard. Historian by profession as a faculty member, historical society director, college president, and presidential library/museum director, he is also a functional father and occasional grandfather.

Maxine Follstad lives in Pelican Lake, Wisconsin. This is her first appearance in a CSS Publications anthology.

J. M. Frank, a graphic designer and art director by profession, has been writing poetry for 25 years. Only two years ago she attempted her first publication; since then, more than 70 of her poems have had acceptance.

Arthur C. Frick is a painter and a professor of art at Wartburg College in Waverly, Iowa.

Kathryn Gelander is a newspaper reporter who enjoys writing poetry. Many of her poems have been published. She has two sons and five grandchildren and continues to work past retirement age.

Michael Gfoeller is a student of Arab culture and politics, as well as German, Arabic, French and English literature. He has been writing poetry for 10 years.

Martha K. Graham is a retired educator now teaching piano and violin. Her interests are writing, nature, research, and a 150-year-old Mississippi River house, the subject of a collection of her poetry. This is her seventh appearance in a CSS Publications anthology.

Tracy Grandy, 19, is a psychology major at the University of Northern Iowa. Besides writing, she enjoys reading, dancing, and drawing. This is her third published poem.

Marie Grant is a published writer of poetry and short stories who spends much of her time giving readings of her poetry and monologues. Marie is a playwright and has had several of her plays produced by a drama club in her community. She has acted in and directed some of her original plays.

Jason Hobson is a third-grader at Platte River Elementary School in Honor, Michigan. He enjoys baseball, camping, swimming, and reading.

Claudia Hochberg is an artist and teacher who has been writing poetry for the past five years. "I enjoy being creative and writing poetry as an outlet for my thoughts and feelings."

Patricia J. Hoad is an executive secretary in Princeton whose leisure time is devoted to poetry and short fiction.

Jessie Eastman Holt, 82, wrote her first poem at age 10. She has lived in many states, including Alaska, and is now at work on a book about life in southwest Wisconsin early in this century.

Frances H. Hughes has been writing poetry since early teens. She is a registered nurse who remains active although past retirement age. A grandmother of two, she lists writing, cooking, and reading as her hobbies.

Renee Ingledue, 26, is married and has two children (Blake, 3½, and Jourdan, 2); she is a part-time secretary. "I have been writing poetry since I was 12. I am an avid reader and plan to write a book."

Sarah Jaquish, 11, has been writing since age nine. She enjoys reading, singing, and acting.

Vernelia B. Jobe is a mother and grandmother who lives on a farm; she and her husband raise feeder pigs. Her hobbies are bird-watching and gardening. She has had some poetry published and sold.

Frances R. Johnson has recently retired from teacher/counselor duties and is moving West. She has had printed an artist proof of photograhy (1984) and poetry expressing the natural beauty of Michigan. Although she has been writing poetry for 18 years, these are her first published poems.

Wilfred M. Johnson is president of the League of Minnesota Poets and memberships chairman of the Southern Minnesota Poets' Society. He is widely published and has received numerous state and national awards for his poetry.

Ann Caroline Kabel, a native Iowan and graduate of the University of Iowa (B.A., M.A., English), currently lives and works in Germany. She writes poetry, heroic fantasy, and science fiction.

Minneh M. Karanja has been a "closet writer" since childhood; this is her first published work. She is a barrister (of Gray's Inn, London) and practices in Nairobi, where she was born 25 years ago.

Jill King loves writing poetry and short stories and delving into history and eastern religions. However, the real loves of her life are her husband and son, Wayne and Judson, and her shaggy dog, Goody Two Shoes. She is a graduate of the University of South Carolina, a former teacher, and a perennial student. Her poetry has been published extensively, and she has been nominated for Poet Laureate of South Carolina.

Pat King writes often about people she loves, some of whom are all over the world. She's interested in the challenge of learning to understand the many cultures of the world, including her own.

Aaron Koch, 15, is in the 10th grade at Carlisle High School in Iowa. Although this is one of Aaron's first poems, he plans to continue to explore his writing potential.

Kim Kolker, 19, is an English major at Pomona College in Claremont, California, who hopes to study abroad at Oxford. She completed her first novel in the fourth grade and nows sticks to poetry.

Meg Kramer, 74, is a retired music/English teacher who began writing poetry as an artistic and emotional outlet when rheumatoid arthritis forced her to give up piano. She had formerly written a newspaper column, *From A Corner Kitchen.*

Sister Monica Lammers, O.S.B., is a retired food service supervisor from St. Mary's Hospital in Detroit Lakes and several other places in Minnesota. She received her high school training at Mount St. Benedict Convent.

Dean M. Le Bel, 31, is a systems analyst, bon vivant, bartender, and active participant in the Soulard Culture Squad, a monthly poetry recital group that meets in Soulard, a historic district of St. Louis.

Dr. E. "Betse" Matthew Lewis has travelled worldwide in her pursuit of adventure at sea, stained glass, computers, and micrographics. Raised in Virginia, she lives on Lake Melva in Florida with her sister Mary Matthew, a prolific poet.

At age 26, ***Ron MacLean's*** goal in life is to be a successful writer by age 25.

Eleanor Mader is a graduate student/teaching assistant in the department of English at Texas A&M University. "I thrive on a diet of aerobics, gardening, quiet summer mornings, and having a husband and daughter who give me the freedom to try my wings."

Janet Marie enjoys tennis, swimming, sailing, and horses. She is an adjunct instructor of writing and writes poetry when at the lake, in the mountains, or by the sea. She directs the Poetry & Prose Series, Arts Council of Princeton.

Barbara McCorkhill has six adult children and one granddaughter. A student at Case Western Reserve University working toward a master's in social work, she has been writing poetry for about eight years.

Mike Mihaljevich, 33, is an unemployed teacher who writes poetry only sporadically. He has been involved for three years working against present U.S. policy in Central America.

Ann Majure is an elementary teacher. She has been writing poetry for only a year, and this is her first published poem.

Marsha A. Mitchell is a mother of three who works for a local investor-owned utility company. She keeps busy following the kids and trying to keep up with her 100-year-old, 11-room house. "I love to write but have found that lately time constraints have slowed me down."

Dorothy Moore, an English major and art special graduate of Ball State University, Muncie, Indiana, makes up poetry while doing household tasks. She loves to cook, sew, do needlepoint, and paint pictures.

Delores Mundell has been writing poetry, short stories, and children's story poems for 40 years. She is currently working on her first full length novel.

LaMoyne Nations says her innate love for poetry blossomed after a friend requested her to write examples of a variety of poems for a "how to" book on poetry, a demanding and enlightening task.

Mary Hamilton Neary started memorizing poetry at Union Point School. A graduate of Friends University, she has a master's degree from WSU.

Beth Helen Nowell, 26, began writing poetry as an exercise in idea expression and thought completion. Since, it has become an implement in the search for a less obvious truth about life.

Nancy Brier O'Neal, 39, is the mother of 2 daughters (ages 9 & 11) who works as a state employee as a driver license clerk in Cuero for the Texas Department of Public Safety. Married to a very talented artist, she has had over 150 poems published nationwide.

Mary Pagliaro, 34, has one son, Paul. She enjoys writing, works as a state senator's sectretary, has an income tax preparation service, and volunteers as a reader for the blind at the University of Wisconsin-Madison.

Kay Logson Pearce, 47, is the wife of Oscar, a chemical salesman, mother of three grown daughters, and grandmother of Tara, 2. She is a daughter in an exceptionally wonderful family. A first grade teacher for 13 years, she has been a lifelong compulsive artist and writer.

Douglas Scott Pfeiffer, 12, has been writing poetry and short stories since the age of 8. In addition, he enjoys music, sports, geology, and computers.

Janet Rahmani, a Drake University graduate, returned to Iowa in 1979 after living 6 years in Israel. She juggles a hectic life as the working mother of 3 lively children and a commitment to her writing.

Dolly Redden is the wife of a retired Air Force pilot and a novice writer whose yearning for expression is beginning to blossom. She's also a Christian speaker for retreats and banquets.

Linda J. Reed, 32, a blue-collar worker, has been writing for 20 years and is now co-authoring a novel based on a Sherlock Holmes character.

Christy Revenell, 10, is in the sixth grade at Platte River School in Honor, Michigan.

William P. Riddle states, "My son was only two and my daughter a mere child of seven when I entered my first CSS Publications Poetry Contest. Now, he is a husky nine year old and she is a young lady of fourteen. My family is growing up with CSS."

Kay Jons Roelfsema teaches creative writing at Eldora-New Providence High School. Besides writing poetry, another favorite activity is running; several of her prize-winning poems were composed while running.

Jennifer Mary Ryan, 10, is a student at Platte River Elementary School. This is her first year for writing poems, and she hopes to pursue this is in her future. Jennifer is also a "Record Eagle" carrier.

Betty Jane Sachara, a Cleveland, Ohio native and graduate of Notre Dame College, transplanted to California in 1957. A former language instructor, she is a Chaparral Poet and World Poetry Society member dedicated to a lifetime of writing.

Lynne Proctor Sancken, 34, is a busy mother of three who still clutches for pen and paper when the spirit moves her. Her favorite writing place is the car.

Jean Marie Schultz has been in love with the printed word since learning to read and considers its use her medium of exchange for the pleasure and gift of life.

June L. Shipley is a member of the Lake County Club and the Indiana State Federation of Poetry Clubs. This is her third appearance in a CSS Publications anthology; she has also appeared in numerous other publications.

IvaNelle Simak gardens, camps, canoes, bird watches, tutors, writes, and enjoys people, especially her family and their families. She is a retired primary room teacher.

Conrad Simonson, wood and wordsmith, also teaches ethics at Luther College. He would write the great American novel, but he doesn't know how, so he pets his dog instead.

Caroline St. Julien, 37, has been studying and writing poetry seriously for 10 years. "I am indebted to three great women poet/friends who have been guiding me. I continue to learn and write."

Jean A. Stanford, 22, has composed poetry since she was a child, but this is her first published poem. She is a manager at a local McDonald's restaurant and writes in her spare time.

Julie Stratton is in the sixth grade at Lathrop Elementary School in Lathrop, California.

Julie Stratton is in the sixth grade at Lathrop Elementary School in Lathrop, California.

Alice Mackenzie Swaim is a member of the Academy of American Poets, Poetry Society of American, and the state poetry societies of California, Kentucky, and New Hampshire. She is the author of 12 books, and of many articles and brochures. She serves as a book reviewer and contest judge.

Justin Mitchell Sytsma, 9, is the son of Alexis Mitchell, a financial planner and artist, and Curt Sytsma, an attorney and poet. Justin's hobbies are long-distance running, baseball, soccer, and other literary endeavors.

Sara Sheppard Szymanski has just finished the first grade and likes to write poetry. ("My mom helps me spell the hard words.") She is also interested in playing T-ball, learning piano and ballet, and reading.

Bonnie L. Thomas is a commercial interior designer. Having always longed to be a writer, too, she began to express herself in poems and has now discovered the value of poetry for self-awareness.

Averi Torres, 42, is a psychic consultant to Malibu's elite, celebrities, and world leaders. Also, she is chairperson of the board of an international trading and investment firm co-founded with husband Dennis.

Dennis Torres, 42, is an international developer, businessman, pilot and adventurer. Poetry is his way of sharing special spiritual moments of his life experience. This is his second appearance in a CSS Publications anthology.

Dorothy J. Turnour lives in Ontario, California. This is her first appearance in a CSS Publications anthology.

Frank Raymond Tropea has an M.A. in literature and psychology from Harvard and hopes one day to teach. "Like Ms. Blanche DuBois, I don't want reality — *I want magic.* So, deep within myself, I reach out for magic and out comes poetry."

Chema Ude, 36, is a career urban planner from eastern Nigeria currently living in Riverside, Calfornia. He has published poems, fiction, and photojournalist materials in Nigeria, West Germany, and in the U.S. He is finishing his first poetry book.

Barbara Kee Vatovec, born in Johnson City, Illinois, is married to Tony and has two daughters, Jennifer and Julie. Her hobbies include reading, music, and writing poetry and songs.

Judith Lewis von Buchler is the mother of two elementary-age school children and a teacher of writing at Anderson College. After intending to write poetry for 20 years, she has now finally begun.

Ann Switzer Walters was born and raised in Flagstaff, Arizona. She has an M.S. degree in exercise physiology from Utah State University and teaches physical education in Gibson City Middle School. She is married to Gerald L. Walters.

Jean Lollich Warner is a former kindergarten teacher who is presently a housewife. She has a B.A. degree from Cornell College in Mt. Vernon, Iowa, and an M.A. degree from Columbia University, New York City. Her hobbies include reading, writing, knitting, and China painting.

Elizabeth Welden, 15, enjoys music, art, and traveling. She is interested in working with underprivileged people after graduation.

Krista Werner, 18, will never be anything more than a poet at heart unless she wins the million-dollar lottery, so she is studying pre-med at Washington University in St. Louis.

Clo Weirich says, "My love of earth, sea, sky, and water builds within me as a 'well' that is a chief source of my inspirations."

Stephen Ray White is a psychology major at a small, private college in Missouri. He enjoys playing chess and considers himself to be a philospher.

Alex A. Widicker, 77, is a retired teacher who loves nature and studies hummingbirds as a hobby. Before stores sold feeders, he made and sold them. This is his first and only poem.

Roger Wilbur has had poetry published nationally since 1972. He's an innovator in the teaching of humanities courses at the college level. An associate professor at Atlanta Junior College, he is well known for his workshops in "humanness."

Glenda Winders teaches at Central Missouri State University. She has published poems, short stories, and essays and is currently at work on a novel. This is her third appearance in a CSS Publications anthology.

Mildred Hope Wood is an author of educational articles and materials and a frequent speaker at international conferences, state conferences, and meetings of various service clubs.

Jeff Wright, 36, is a school teacher. He and his wife have three children.

Mary Himka Young, 28, is a working mother who nowadays writes for relaxation. She first began dabbling with poetry and songwriting at age 12. She works as a circulation clerk for Observer/Eccentric newspapers in Livonia, Michigan.

Karla J. Ziesemer, 37, has been writing poetry for 20 years. She is an emergency nurse specialist and is head nurse of emergency at Beatrice Community Hospital. Special interests include expressive arts and outdoor adventuring.

Other Books By CSS Publications

A Hook In Its Mouth, *Poems by Sarah P. Simmons* (1984)
The Rhyme & Reason of Curt Sytsma (1982)
Profiles Cut from the Wave (1983)
The Whisper of Dreams (1982)
Images of Our Lives (1981)
Moments in Time (1980)
Feelings (1979)
Emotions, Emotions (1978)

About the Publisher

CSS Publications was conceived and founded by C. Sherman Severin and Rebecca S. Bell in 1977. It was dedicated at birth to the vitality of the small press movement.

Through the publication of seven annual poetry anthologies and the highly acclaimed hardcover book, *The Rhyme & Reason of Curt Sytsma,* CSS Publications has acquired a national reputation as a respected publisher of poetry.

In its unique system, CSS Publications sponsors annual poetry contests based on the theme of "human emotions." The contests are open to individuals of all ages and from every state in the nation, as well as to persons living anywhere in the world.

Poems entered in the contests are evaluated by a panel of judges consisting of poets and English professors. Through a two-step procedure, judges select poems to be included in the current book and determine the prize-winning entries. The top five poems earn cash awards, and several other poems receive honorable mention. Published poets are given a complimentary copy of the book and their hometown newspapers are informed of their achievement.

All poets who enter the contests are invited to the annual Poetry Day & Awards Banquet. Master of ceremonies for the event is Curt L. Sytsma, the Des Moines attorney whose poetry appears in syndication in newspapers across the country. The 1984 Banquet is scheduled for September 29, 1984, in Des Moines, Iowa. The featured poet is Sarah P. Simmons, author of *A Hook in Its Mouth.*

For additional information about CSS Publications, write to:
> CSS Publications
> P.O. Box 23
> Iowa Falls, Iowa 50126